CONTENT AREA ESL: SOCIAL STUDIES

Dennis Terdy

Linda Mrowicki,
Developmental Editor

Linmore Publishing, Inc.

P.O. Box 1545   Palatine, IL 60078

(815) 223-7499

Linmore Publishing, Inc.
P.O. Box 1545
Palatine, IL 60078

© Linmore Publishing, Inc. 1986 **Updated 1993**
First printing, 1986 Printed in the United States of America

CONTENT AREA ESL: SOCIAL STUDIES
ISBN 0-916591-06-9

ACKNOWLEDGEMENTS

I would like to thank the following people for their valuable comments and suggestions for this text: **David Barker,** Main East High School, IL; **Terri Corasanti Dale,** Center For Applied Linguistics; **Maria Impink Hernandez,** National Clearinghouse for Bilingual Education; **Sharon Huck,** Glenbard North High School, IL; **Sue Morrisroe,** Main West High School, IL; and **Cindy Zucker,** Chicago Public Schools and Joann Holba, Arbor School District, IL.

I would also like to express my thanks to **Linda Mrowicki,** the developmental editor, who used her expertise in ESL to help conceptualize the approach and organize the scope and content. Her ability to produce ESL textbooks was vital in transforming my "teacher worksheets" into a real book!

I would like to make a special dedication:

   To my children for all the Saturday morning cartoons I missed!

   To my wife for the infinite patience, support, and "shared" family responsibilities that helped me with this project!

   To my parents for the enthusiasm, drive, and persistence!

Dennis Terdy

INTRODUCTION

CONTENT AREA ESL: SOCIAL STUDIES is written for intermediate level Limited English Proficient (LEP) students at the secondary level. It prepares students with the skills and strategies needed to effectively transition to "regular" content area classroom instruction. The text is also appropriate for university level students who need to improve their reading and writing skills for entry into academic instruction and Adult Education students who need to improve their reading skills and knowledge about U.S. history in order to obtain their GED.

CONTENT AREA ESL: SOCIAL STUDIES can be used in a variety of classroom situations: 1). as a core text in a special purpose ESL class 2). as a supplementary text in a multi-purpose ESL class 3). as a core text in a "sheltered" social studies class or 4). as a study guide in a regular social studies class.

CONTENT AREA ESL: SOCIAL STUDIES represents a new, integrative approach to teaching English as a Second Language. LEP students, especially at the secondary level, need this approach to successfully transition to the mainstream content area classes. This text provides students with vocabulary and grammatical structure practice in a social studies context and the reading and writing skills necessary for functioning in a regular social studies curriculum.

RATIONALE
Secondary LEP students are often expected to function in a regular social studies class, yet they are seldom provided with the appropriate language skills needed to use the regular social studies materials. Existing general purpose ESL texts do not fully develop the specific reading and writing skills relevant to social studies. CONTENT AREA ESL: SOCIAL STUDIES utilizes a highly integrative language learning format which addresses social studies specific needs with:

- essential textbook reading skills and strategies
- content reading passages appropriate to students' cultural backgrounds and reading levels
- recognition and integration of background knowledge and information as it directly applies to content area reading
- comprehension questions which cover six levels of information processing
- essential grammar study which significantly enhances the development of writing skills
- writing activities with guided questions which cover a variety of perspectives and rhetorical areas.
- graphical literacy skills for comprehension of high level content information found in social studies materials.

CONTENT
CONTENT AREA ESL: SOCIAL STUDIES contains eighteen lessons. Each lesson consists of a pre-reading exercise, a two page reading passage, a vocabulary exercise, a reading comprehension exercise, a grammar exercise, graphical literacy exercise, a writing exercise, and a review exercise.

Pre-reading Exercise
Reflecting current research in reading (Goodman, 1967; Smith, 1971; and Carrel, 1983), CONTENT AREA ESL: SOCIAL STUDIES integrates the role of personal experience and schema into its approach through four activities:
1. **Personal Survey** consists of questions which the teacher and students discuss prior to reading the passage. These questions focus students' attention on personal experiences and knowledge about the lesson topic.
2. **Pre-reading** provides a brief overview which focusses students on the reading.
3. **Content vocabulary** lists a few key social studies terms found in the reading and which students are likely to have some knowledge about. Discussing these words prior to the reading brings out students' knowledge, experiences, and ideas about the topic.
4. **Survey** integrates content area reading components of Robinson's SQRRR (Survey, question, read, recite, review, 1947) and Auckerman's survey techniques (1972). Students use these strategies to find answers to general questions prior to the actual reading. The survey techniques progressively expand from the initial surveying of the subtitles in the initial lessons to surveying of the first paragraph, subtitles, words in bold print, pictures, and summary paragraph in the final lessons.

Reading Passage

Each lesson has a two page reading passage written for second language learners at the high beginning or intermediate levels. These passages provide a social studies context in which to study the language. They are NOT intended to be concise, detailed descriptions of historical events. These passages focus on different areas of social studies - history, geography, sociology, and American government. They have been selected because of their important historical and cultural insights.

Vocabulary Exercise

This exercise develops students' vocabulary by focussing on non-technical words which occur frequently in a social studies context. Examples of such words are: "equal", "discovery", and "discrimination". This vocabulary practice is presented in three ways: 1). matching words with definitions 2). completing cloze sentences and 3). using word parts (prefixes, suffixes, etc.) to establish the meaning of words.

Comprehension Exercise

Each lesson contains questions which reflect six different levels of processing according to Bloom's Taxonomy: knowledge, comprehension, application, analysis, synthesis, and evaluation Many of these types of questions are found in regular social studies textbooks but seldom included in LEP reading exercises.

Grammar Exercise

This exercise reinforces students' knowledge of grammar and practices it in a social studies context. The text does not attempt to teach grammar; rather it REINFORCES and PROVIDES PRACTICE in grammar points critical to social studies. Research indicates four major high frequency grammar areas in regular social studies texts: verb tenses (usually past tense, positive and negative), pronoun referents, prepositional phrases (usually time phrases) and connecting words (both conjunctions and transitional adverbs). CONTENT AREA ESL: SOCIAL STUDIES contains a four phase activity in each lesson 1). students review the grammar point by reading the grammar box 2). students re-read the passage to find examples of the grammar point 3). students produce the grammatical structure in a sentence related to the social studies topic and 4). students create one or two sentences with the grammatical structure in the social studies context.

Graphical Literacy

This exercise develops the necessary skills for comprehending typical charts and graphs found in social studies texts: **maps** with labels, shaded areas, symbols, and keys; **timelines** with events and dates; **diagrams** (visual representations of a structure or process); **charts** (a verbal summary); **tables** (information presented in rows and columns); and a variety of **graphs** - pie graphs, horizontal and vertical bar graphs, pictographs, and line graphs. Each lesson contains a graph or chart which either summarizes important information in the lesson or extends the lesson by adding other relevant information. These graphical items are presented in a sequenced fashion which allows progressive skill development. The graphical item is followed by questions which focus students' attention on the STRUCTURE of the graph and the INFORMATION contained in the graph.

Writing Exercise

These activities are specifically designed to prepare students to write short essays or reports often required in the regular content area texts. The writing activities focus on different rhetorical styles frequently encountered in social studies: description, cause-effect, comparison/contrast, persuasion, and chronological order. Pre-writing activities have been integrated to prepare students for the actual extended writing. The pre-writing consists of guided questions which students brainstorm possible answers to. After students discuss and write their answers, the exercise directs them to develop their answers into a paragraph or paragraphs.

Each writing task is designed to make the content area writing task interesting and even fun. Frequently the exercises take the information from the reading passage and directs students to evaluate it by writing opinions or by taking a role to express a particular point of view. For example, in the lesson "Early Settlers", students take the role of an early settler and write a letter to a family member explaining the problems of life in the New World.

Review Exercise

This exercise presents the key events and individuals from the lesson. The students are asked to recall the information and explain the significance of each individual or event. This summary integrates the study skill of reviewing while giving the students a feeling of accomplishment in having learned some historical information.

Chapter Review
At the end of each chapter students identify major events for designated years and describe the significance of key names, places, and events. These reviews summarize the major events of the time period and assist students in developing reviewing skills.

SUGGESTED METHODOLOGY
The following steps are recommended for successful use of the text. Because teachers have different teaching styles and students have a variety of learning styles, each teacher should feel free to adapt the text to best meet the needs of his or her students.

Pre-reading Exercise.
Personal Survey: Ask the questions and lead students in a discussion. An alternative activity is to divide students into pairs and have them ask each other the questions and report the answers back to the class.

Pre-reading: Read the introduction to the class.

Content Vocabulary: Ask individual students to report what they know about each of the words. The actual words and the information may be recorded on the blackboard for later reference.

Survey: Ask the questions and direct students' attention to the designated item to be surveyed, such as the subtitles and the initial paragraph. After surveying, ask students to make predictions about the content of the lesson. Ask students to read the comprehension questions and to try to find the answers as they read the passage.

Reading Passage. Students read the passage silently in class or as homework. Answer any general questions students may have after they have read the passage. A teacher may elect to have individual students read the passage aloud to note miscues which identify problems in comprehension.

Comprehension Questions. Explain the directions to the students. Indicate that some questions require an opinion or inference based on the reading content. Students should answer the questions silently and later review their answers in class.

Grammar Exercise. Briefly review the grammatical structure. The teacher may choose to supplement the text material by further oral or written practice of the structure depending on the students' needs. Students should complete the exercises silently and individually.

Graphical Literacy. Introduce the graphical item by asking students general questions about the structure and content of the graph. Students silently and individually answer the questions.

Writing Exercise. In the pre-writing phase, ask the questions and lead students in a discussion of possible answers. Students should write their own answers to the questions. Review individual students' answers so that appropriate content and form exist. Students, then, use their answers to write a paragraph or paragraphs. The actual writing is then reviewed and corrected by the teacher.

With respect to spelling, punctuation, and grammar errors, teachers must use their own judgement in determining which errors should be corrected and how they should be corrected. This purpose of this exercise is to develop writing fluency. Over-correction may hinder some students' writing fluency. On the other hand, under-correction may encourage other students to write fluently, yet incomprehensibly due to the large number of errors.

Review Exercise. Ask students about the historical significance of the items listed. Answers may be noted on the blackboard.

CONTENT AREA ESL: SOCIAL STUDIES SYLLABUS

	LESSON	GRAMMAR FOCUS	WRITING FOCUS	GRAPHICAL LITERACY FOCUS
UNIT ONE	1. Native Americans	Past tense, regular and irregular	Description	Map with labels
	2. Early Settlers	Past tense, positive and negative	Cause-Effect	Map with shaded areas
	3. The War of Independence	Pronouns and their referents	Cause-Effect Chronology	Map with labels, key, and chart
	4. A Nation Begins	Connectors - "and", "but"	Description Chronology	Diagram
UNIT TWO	5. Westward Expansion	Connectors - "however", "in fact", "therefore"	Description	Map with routes
	6. The North and the South	Comparative adjectives	Comparison/contrast	Bar charts
	7. The Civil War	Pronoun referents	Chronology Description	Map with labels, key, and table
	8. The Reunited Country Grows	Past tense, positive and negative	Description Cause-Effect	Pictograph
UNIT THREE	9. Industrial Expansion	Time phrases - "in", "on", "for", "during" Superlative adjectives	Description Cause-Effect	Pictograph
	10. Early Immigration	Clause connectors - "that", "who", "which" in subject position	Cause-Effect	pie graphs
	11. World War I	Pronoun referents	Cause-Effect	Timelines
	12. Good Times and Bad Times	Connectors - "because", "because of"	Cause-Effect	Line graph
UNIT FOUR	13. The New Deal	Clause connectors - "that", "who", "which" in object	Description	Table
	14. World War II	Connectors - "before", "after", "during", "until", "while"	Cause-Effect	Timelines
	15. The United Nations	Passive voice	Persuasion	Diagram
UNIT FIVE	16. The Country Prospers	Review: Clause connectors	Description	Bar chart
	17. The Struggle for Civil Rights	Review: Connectors	Cause-Effect	Line graph
	18. The U.S. Today		Persuasion	Bar, pie graphs

© Linmore Publishing, Inc. 1986   P.O. Box 1545   Palatine, IL 60078

CONTENTS

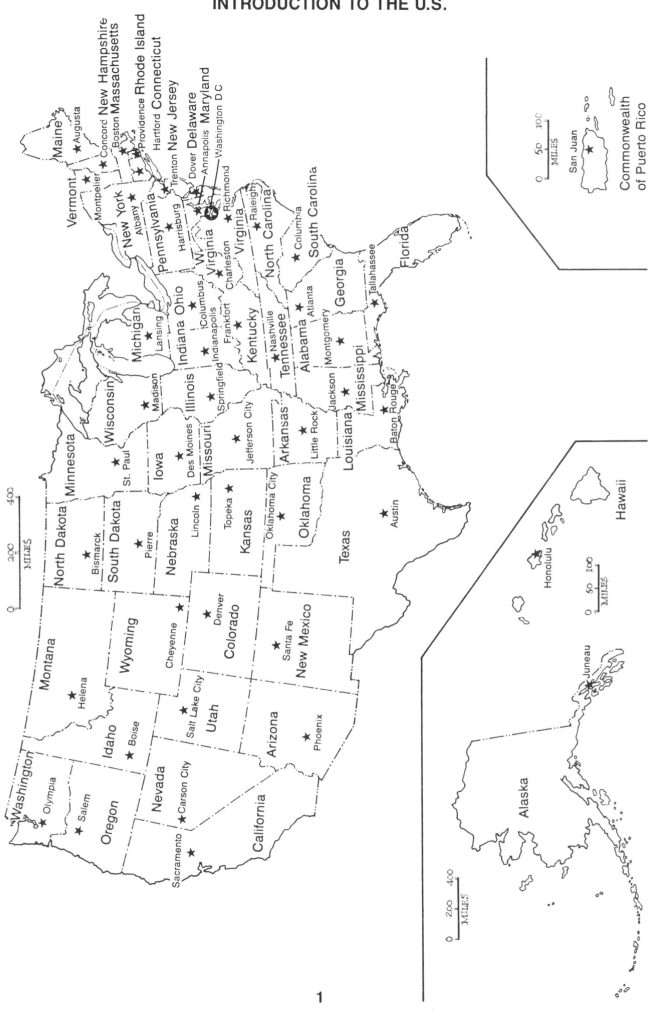

GRAPHICAL LITERACY.
Look at the map. Answer the questions.

1. Find your state. Circle it.

2. What is the capital of your state?_____

3. Find California. Is it in the east or in the west?_____

4. Find New York. Is it in the west or in the east?_____

5. Find Florida. Is it in the east or in the west?_____

6. Find Washington. Is it in the east or in the west?_____

7. Find Nevada. Is it in the east or in the west?_____

8. Find Texas. Is it in the north or in the south?_____

9. Find Georgia. Is it in the north or in the south?_____

10. Find Illinois. Is it an eastern, western, or central state?_____

11. Find New Jersey. Is it an eastern, western, or central state?_____

12. Which state is north of Wyoming?_____

13. Which state is south of Utah?_____

14. Which state is east of Kansas?_____

15. Which state is west of Nevada?_____

16. Which state is west of Ohio?_____

17. What is the capital of Colorado?_____

18. What is the capital of Hawaii?_____

19. What is the capital of Minnesota?_____

20. What is the capital of Alaska?_____

21. What is the capital of Michigan?_____

22. What is the capital of Delaware?_____

23. What is the capital of Iowa? _____

24. What is the capital of North Dakota? _____

25. What is the capital of Arizona? _____

26. What is the capital of Oregon? _____

27. What is the capital of Virginia? _____

28. What is the capital of Massachusetts? _____

ABBREVIATION	STATE	CAPITAL
AL	Alabama	Montgomery
AK	Alaska	Juneau
AZ	Arizona	Phoenix
AR	Arkansas	Little Rock
CA	California	Sacramento
CO	Colorado	Denver
CT	Connecticut	Hartford
DE	Delaware	Dover
FL	Florida	Tallahassee
GA	Georgia	Atlanta
HI	Hawaii	Honolulu
ID	Idaho	Boise
IL	Illinois	Springfield
IN	Indiana	Indianapolis
IA	Iowa	Des Moines
KS	Kansas	Topeka
KY	Kentucky	Frankfort
LA	Louisiana	Baton Rouge
ME	Maine	Augusta
MD	Maryland	Annapolis
MA	Massachusetts	Boston
MI	Michigan	Lansing
MN	Minnesota	St. Paul
MS	Mississippi	Jackson
MO	Missouri	Jefferson City
MT	Montana	Helena
NE	Nebraska	Lincoln
NV	Nevada	Carson City
NH	New Hampshire	Concord
NJ	New Jersey	Trenton
NM	New Mexico	Santa Fe
NY	New York	Albany
NC	North Carolina	Raleigh
ND	North Dakota	Bismarck
OH	Ohio	Columbus
OK	Oklahoma	Oklahoma City
OR	Oregon	Salem
PA	Pennsylvania	Harrisburg
RI	Rhode Island	Providence
SC	South Carolina	Columbia
SD	South Dakota	Pierre
TN	Tennessee	Nashville
TX	Texas	Austin
UT	Utah	Salt Lake City
VT	Vermont	Montpelier
VA	Virginia	Richmond
WA	Washington	Olympia
WV	West Virginia	Charleston
WI	Wisconsin	Madison
WY	Wyoming	Cheyenne
PR	Commonwealth of Puerto Rico	San Juan

GRAPHICAL LITERACY.
Look at the table. Answer the questions.

1. What is in the left column?_____

2. What is in the middle column?_____

3. What is in the right column?_____

4. What is the abbreviation for Arkansas?_____

5. What is the abbreviation for Maryland?_____

6. What is the abbreviation for North Carolina?_____

7. What is the abbreviation for Pennsylvania?_____

8. Which state is MI?_____

9. Which state is AL?_____

10. Which state is OK?_____

11. Which state is NH?_____

12. What is the capital of RI?_____

13. What is the capital of KY?_____

14. What is the capital of TN?_____

15. What is the abbreviation for West Virginia?_____

16. What is the abbreviation for Puerto Rico?_____

17. Which state is MO?_____

18. What is the capital of Vermont?_____

19. Which state is CT?_____

20. What is the capital of MS?_____

21. Which state is WI?_____

22. Which state is SC?_____

23. What is the capital of New York?_____

24. Which state is NM?_____

25. Which state is LA?_____

26. What is the abbreviation for Rhode Island?_____

27. What is the capital of Indiana?_____

28. What is the capital of the U.S.?_____

WRITING ACTIVITY.
Answer the questions with complete sentences.

1. What is the name of your city, town or rural area?

_____

2. Which state do you live in?

_____

3. What is the capital of your state?

_____

4. Is your state in the Northeastern, Southeastern, Middle, Northwestern, or Southwestern part of the United States?

_____

5. What states are close to your state?

_____

_____

Describe where you live. Use your answers from the above questions to write a paragraph. The title should be: I Live In The United States.

_____

_____

_____

_____

_____

_____

_____

_____

_____

_____

_____

_____

_____

UNIT ONE

NATIVE AMERICANS

EARLY SETTLERS

THE WAR OF INDEPENDENCE

A NATION BEGINS

NATIVE AMERICANS

PERSONAL SURVEY
Discuss these questions with your teacher and class.

1. Who were the first people to come to North America?
2. Where did these people live?
3. How did they live?

PRE-READING

Many people were in North America before the Europeans came. These people had their own languages and cultures. You will read about them in this lesson.

CONTENT VOCABULARY
These words are important in this lesson. What do you know about them?

Native Americans
tribes

SURVEY
Read the subtitles. Read the subtitles and look at the pictures.

Who were the major groups of North Americans?

Look at the comprehension questions. Try to find the answers to these questions when you read the passage.

NATIVE AMERICANS

The Native Americans had many different cultures, religions, and languages. They made tools and grew food. They had organized **societies.** Each society made rules. People did different kinds of work in these societies. Some people were farmers, some were hunters, and others were craftsmen. There were many groups of Native Americans. They lived in all parts of North America.

Winter home of the Fox.

The Southeastern Tribes
The Southeastern tribes were in the Southeastern United States. They lived in such states as Mississippi, Georgia, Alabama, and Florida. Some of the tribes included the Creek, Chickasaw, and Choctaw. These tribes fished and hunted. The women owned the land. The men were the heads of the families.

The Algonkians
The Algonkians lived in an area from northern Canada to North and South Carolina. Some of the tribes included the Massachusetts, Pequot, and Mohegans. These Native Americans were hunters and farmers. They planted corn. They lived in villages. They made pottery and baskets. They also used valuable shells for money. Their money was called *chief (a leader)* **wampum.** Each tribe had a chief. Each chief inherited his position from his father.

The Iroquois
The Iroquois settled in the forests of such states as New York, Pennsylvania, and Ohio. Three of these tribes were the Mohawks, Oneidas, and Senecas. The Iroquois tribes were farmers. They grew corn, beans, and squash. They fished and hunted deer. They built large houses. Several families lived in a house.

Salish Indian grave post.

Two Indians hunting a buffalo.

The Tribes of the Western Great Lakes

These tribes lived in such states as Michigan, Minnesota, Illinois, and Wisconsin. Three of these tribes were the Sauk, Kaskaskia, Fox, and Peoria. The men were hunters. The women grew corn and other vegetables. Many tribes had summer houses and winter houses.

The Native Americans of the Plains

The Great Plains of the United States include an area from Oklahoma to North Dakota. Some Plains tribes were the Dakota, Cheyenne, Crow, and Blackfoot. These tribes had horses. They hunted buffalo.

The Northwest Tribes

These tribes settled in states such as Oregon and Washington. Three tribes were the Tillamook, Nootka, and Salish. They fished for salmon. They built tall carved statues called **totem poles.** A totem pole identified and protected the family.

The Southwest Tribes

The land of the Southwest includes Nevada, Arizona, New Mexico, and Colorado. Major Southwest tribes include the Pueblos, Hopi, Navajos, and Apaches. The tribes were very different in this region. The Pueblos were farmers. They grew cotton and made clothes. The Navajos were farmers, too. They raised animals like sheep, goats, and cattle. The Apaches were good warriors. They were brave fighters.

Summary

The Native Americans had different languages and cultures. Each group had its own way of life. When the Europeans arrived, the lives of the Native Americans began to change. These changes threatened the cultures and lives of all the Native Americans in North America.

VOCABULARY EXERCISE
Read these words. Write the words next to their definitions.

a farmer   a hunter   a chief   a society   to inherit   a tribe

1. _____ The leader of a North American tribe.

2. _____ A person who grows food.

3. _____ A group of people who make rules and follow them.

4. _____ To get something from one's parents when they die.

5. _____ A group of Native Americans.

6. _____ A person who kills animals for food.

COMPREHENSION EXERCISE.
Answer the questions.

1. Identify four groups of Native Americans.

_____

_____

2. Identify a tribe which lived in the Northwest.

_____

3. Describe one Native American culture.

_____

_____

4. What did the Algonkians use for money?

_____

5. Why do you think the Fox had summer houses and winter houses?

_____

_____

6. What did totem poles mean to the Northwest tribes?

_____

_____

7. How were the Apaches and Pueblos different?

_____

_____

GRAMMAR EXERCISE.

```
┌─────────────────────────────────────────────────────────┐
│                                                           │
│   PAST TENSE OF REGULAR AND IRREGULAR VERBS               │
│                                                           │
│      For regular verbs: Add "d" or "ed" to the verbs.     │
│      Examples: live - lived and call - called             │
│                                                           │
│      For irregular verbs: Change the form of the verb.    │
│      Examples: come - came and make - made                │
│                                                           │
└─────────────────────────────────────────────────────────┘
```

A. Read the passage. Write the present and past tense of five regular and five irregular verbs.

Regular Present

_____

_____

_____

_____

_____

Regular Past

_____

_____

_____

_____

_____

Irregular Present

_____

_____

_____

_____

Irregular Past

_____

_____

_____

_____

B. Write the past tense of these verbs.

Present	Past
are	_____
begin	_____
build	_____
grow	_____
have	_____
hunt	_____
live	_____
make	_____
raise	_____
speak	_____
use	_____

C. Complete the sentences by writing the correct verb. Use each verb only one time. Remember to use the past tense!

hunt   make   live   speak   have   grow   use   begin   are   build   raise

1. Seven major groups of Native Americans _____ in North America.

2. The Native Americans _____ many different cultures.

3. The tribes _____ different languages.

4. The Algonkians _____ pottery, _____

    corn, and _____ valuable shells for money.

5. The Iroquois _____ farmers.

6. The Cheyenne _____ buffalo.

7. The Tillamook _____ tall totems.

8. The Navajos _____ animals.

9. When the Europeans arrived, the lives of the Native Americans _____ to change.

D. Write two sentences in the past tense. Use information from this lesson.

1. _____

2. _____

13

GRAPHICAL LITERACY.
Look at the map. Answer the questions.

SOME NATIVE AMERICAN GROUPS

1. Where did the Mohawk tribe live?

_____

2. Where did the Hopi tribe live?

_____

3. Where did the Fox tribe live?

_____

4. Where did the Tillamook tribe live?

_____

5. Which Native Americans lived in your state?

_____

6. Do you know the names of other Native American tribes?

_____

WRITING ACTIVITY.
Answer the questions with complete sentences.

1. What is one major Native American group?

_____

2. Where did this group live?

_____

3. Which tribes belonged to this group?

_____

_____

4. How did these tribes live?

_____

_____

_____

Describe one major Native American group. Use your answers to the above questions to write a paragraph. The title of your paragraph should be: A Major Native American Group.

_____

_____

_____

_____

_____

_____

_____

_____

_____

REVIEW EXERCISE.
Do you remember the meaning of the following words?
Native Americans, societies, tribes, totems

EARLY SETTLERS

PERSONAL SURVEY
Discuss these questions with your teacher and class.

1. What country were you born in?
2. When did your family come to the U.S.?
3. Why did your family come to the U.S.?
4. Many people came to North America in the 1600's. Why do you think they came?

PRE-READING

Many Europeans came to North America in the 1600's. They came for different reasons. You will read about these reasons in this lesson.

CONTENT VOCABULARY
These words are important in this lesson. What do you know about them?

Colonies
Pilgrims
Mayflower

SURVEY

Read the subtitles and look at the picture.

Which European countries started colonies in North America in the 1600's?

Look at the comprehension questions. Try to find the answers to these questions when you read the passage.

EARLY SETTLERS

Many Europeans came to North America between the 1500's and 1700's. They came from Spain, France, the Netherlands, and England. The early explorers looked for gold and silver. Other people came to establish colonies.

establish
(to start)

Early settlers landing in North America.

The Spanish Colonies

Christopher Columbus brought the first Spanish ship to North America on October 12, 1492. Some people say that he discovered America, but the Native Americans were in North America before Columbus. Leif Eriksson from Norway also came to North America before Columbus, but settlers did not follow Eriksson.

Many Spanish explorers came after Columbus. They looked for gold and silver. They traveled through the southern part of the United States and northern Mexico in the 1500's and 1600's. They called this land "New Spain". Many Spanish settlers came to New Spain. They established missions for the Catholic Church. They established important cities. One of these cities is St. Augustine, Florida.

The French Colonies

The French began to come to North America in the 1500's. The French came to Canada. They founded important cities like Montreal and Quebec. Quebec was the first French settlement in North America. Quebec was an important trading center located on the St. Lawrence River. The French were involved in fur trading. They traveled on the rivers and lakes. They trapped animals for their furs.

The French traveled down the Mississippi River. They established new **settlements** on the Mississippi River. These settlements included St. Louis, Missouri; Natchez, Mississippi; and New Orleans, Louisiana.

The English Colonies

In 1607, a group of English settlers came to North America. They began a settlement at **Jamestown, Virginia.** Captain John Smith was their leader. The settlers learned to live and trade with the Indians.

In 1619, England allowed the people of Virginia to elect representatives. These representatives were called the **House of Burgesses.** They made new laws. In this year, the first black men and women came to North America. These Blacks were not slaves. They were **indentured servants.** People brought indentured servants to North America to work. The indentured servants were not paid for their work. After they worked for several years, they became free.

elect (to choose)

In 1620, a group of **Pilgrims** arrived in a ship called the Mayflower. They established a settlement at Plymouth, Massachusetts. The Pilgrims came to North America for religious freedom. They were Protestants. They did not agree with the religious practices and beliefs of the Church of England. The Puritan leaders decided to have their own government. They prepared the **Mayflower Compact.** This document had the rules and laws for the new settlement.

In 1630, more ships arrived from England. More than 1000 settlers came to America. These settlers were called **Puritans.** They came because they wanted religious freedom, too. They established the **Massachusetts Bay Colony.**

In 1634, Lord Baltimore founded **Maryland.** Many Catholics settled Maryland. They wanted religious freedom. Other settlers also came to Maryland for religious freedom. The settlers also had the right to help make the laws.

The Dutch Colonies

In 1609, Henry Hudson sailed into New York Bay. He claimed this land for his country, the Netherlands. Dutch settlers began to arrive in 1624. This colony was called **New Netherland.**

Summary

Many Europeans came to North America. Each group settled in a different place. Many settlers came for religious freedom. Many wanted to make their own laws.

VOCABULARY EXERCISE

A. Read these words. Write the words next to their definitions.

to found   to establish   to elect   a representative   an indentured servant   a colony

1. _____ To establish a city.

2. _____ To choose a leader.

3. _____ People choose this person to make laws.

4. _____ To begin something.

5. _____ A settlement which is a part of another country.

6. _____ A person who works without a salary. After a few years, the person becomes free.

B. Read these words. Write the correct form of the words in the sentences.

to settle (verb)   a settler (noun)   a settlement (noun)

1. Henry Hudson established a _____.

2. Many _____ came to North America for religious freedom.

3. The Spanish _____ in the southern part of the United States.

COMPREHENSION EXERCISE.
Answer the questions.

1. Which countries sent settlers to North America?

_____

2. Why did the French come to North America?

_____

3. Why did the Spanish come to North America?

_____

4. Why did the Puritans come to North America?

_____

5. Why is the Mayflower Compact important?

_____

_____

6. Do you think that all the colonies had religious freedom?

_____

_____

7. Where was Henry Hudson from?

_____

GRAMMAR EXERCISE.

NEGATIVE, PAST TENSE

Use NOT after the verb "be" and after "could".
Examples: were - were not and could - could not

Use DID NOT before all other verbs. Remember to change the verb form!
Examples: live - did not live and came - did not come

A. Read the passage. Find five positive past tense verbs. Write them below. Write their negative past tense forms.

Positive Past Tense	Negative Past Tense
_____	_____
_____	_____
_____	_____
_____	_____
_____	_____

B. Read these verbs. Write their negative past tense forms.

agreed   _____

began   _____

came   _____

elected   _____

established   _____

looked   _____

settled   _____

was   _____

C. Complete the sentences by writing the correct verb. Use the verbs listed in Part A. Use either the positive or negative past tense form!

1. Many Europeans _____ to North America.

2. The Spanish settlers _____ for gold in New Spain.

3. The French _____ New Spain.

4. The French _____ in Quebec.

5. Quebec _____ the first French settlement in North America.

6. St. Louis _____ the first French settlement.

7. The English settlers _____ to North America for religious reasons.

8. The Pilgrims _____ with the Church of England.

9. The English settlers _____ Jamestown.

10. The people of Jamestown _____ representatives.

11. Dutch settlers _____ to arrive in 1624.

D. Write one sentence with a positive past tense verb form and one sentences with a negative past tense verb form.

1. _____

2. _____

GRAPHICAL LITERACY.
Look at the map. Answer the questions.

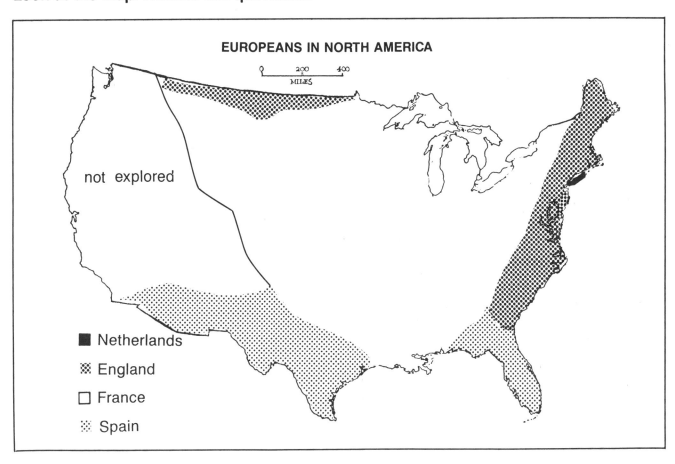

EUROPEANS IN NORTH AMERICA

not explored

■ Netherlands

▨ England

☐ France

▒ Spain

1. Which European countries are shown on the map?

_____

_____

2. Did the Spanish settle in the North or South? _____

3. Did the English settle in the East or in the West? _____

4. Did the Dutch have a large settlement? _____

5. What are some present day states that England settled?

_____

6. What are some present day states that France settled?

_____

7. Name one present day state that Spain settled.

_____

8. Which country had the largest claim? _____

WRITING ACTIVITY.
Answer the questions with complete sentences.

1. Why did the Spanish come to North America?

_____

_____

2. Why did the French come to North America?

_____

_____

3. Why did the English come to North America?

_____

_____

Pretend it is 1615. You arrived in North America six months ago from either Spain, France, or England. You want to stay in North America. Write a letter to your family. Describe your life. Describe the people, opportunities, and daily activities. Explain why you want to stay.

May 21, 1615

Dear _____,

_____

_____

_____

_____

_____

_____

_____

_____

_____

_____

REVIEW EXERCISE.
Do you remember the meaning of the following words?
Colonies, Christopher Columbus, Jamestown, House of Burgesses, indentured servants, Pilgrims, Mayflower Compact

THE WAR OF INDEPENDENCE

PERSONAL SURVEY
Discuss these questions with your teacher and class.

1. What do you think independent means?
2. Why do people want to be independent?
3. Is independence important to you and your family? Why?
4. Is freedom important? How does a person feel if he or she is not free?

PRE-READING

There are many reasons why the War of Independence happened. You will read about the reasons and the important events in this lesson.

CONTENT VOCABULARY
These words are important in this lesson. What do you know about them?

War of Independence
George Washington
Boston Tea Party
Declaration of Independence

SURVEY

Read the subtitles and look at the pictures.

What were the major events of the War of Independence?

Look at the comprehension questions. Try to find the answers to these questions when you read the passage.

THE WAR OF INDEPENDENCE

England had thirteen colonies in the 1700's. France owned land in the west. Many colonists moved west. The French and the English did not get along well. Soon there was war between France and England. This was was called the French and Indian War because England and the colonists fought both the French and the Native Americans. After several years of fighting, the French lost. England won all of France's land east of the Mississippi River.

England Makes Unpopular Laws

debt (money owed)

The English had many war debts from the French and Indian War. England made laws to get money to pay these debts. These laws were called acts. Three acts greatly angered the Colonists. The first act was called the **Sugar Act of 1764.** This act placed a tax on sugar and other products. The colonists had to pay more money for these products. **The Currency Act of 1764** prevented the Colonists from printing their own money. The Colonists had to use English money. The third act was the **Quartering Act of 1765.** This act required the Colonists to provide housing and food for the English Army.

prevent (to stop)

resist (to fight against)

The Colonists resisted these Acts. England sent more soldiers to enforce the new laws. In 1773, the **Tea Act** was passed. This law put a tax on tea. The Colonists were very angry. One night, some Colonists went aboard an English ship in the Boston Harbor. The Colonists threw all the tea into the water! This was called the **Boston Tea Party.**

The Colonists Meet

In 1774, representatives from the thirteen colonies met in Philadelphia. This was called the **First Continental Congress.** The representatives wanted to discuss the taxes and other problems with England. They wrote a letter to the King of England. They asked for many rights. They said, "No taxation without representation". The colonists were not ready to fight for independence. They only wanted more freedom.

"The British are coming!"

The War of Independence Begins in 1775

ammunition (gun power and bullets)

The problems between England and the colonies became worse. In 1775, the Colonists had a large amount of ammunition in Concord, Massachusetts. The English came to take this ammunition. Paul Revere rode through the nearby towns. He announced, "The British are coming!" to the Colonists. A small Colonist army met the English at Lexington, Massachusetts. They fired the first shots of the War of Independence! These were known as "the shots heard around the world".

Surrender at Yorktown

The Declaration of Independence

The Second Continental Congress met soon after the first battles. The representatives decided to fight against England. They chose George Washington as the leader of the army. The army was called the Continental Army. Many colonists volunteered to fight the English.

After one year of fighting, the representatives decided to declare independence from England. Thomas Jefferson wrote the Declaration of Independence. On July 4, 1776, all the colonies adopted the **Declaration of Independence.**

The War Ends in 1781

The war continued in all the colonies. France helped the Colonists. The English defeated Washington's army at Brandywine and Germantown. His army spent the winter of 1777-1778 at Valley Forge, Pennsylvania. The winter was very hard. The army did not have enough food, clothing, or equipment. They continued to fight in 1779 and 1780. On October 19, 1781, the Continental Army defeated the English at Yorktown, Virginia. England surrendered. Two years later England signed a peace treaty. England finally recognized the United States of America as an independent country!

Summary

The Colonies fought the War of Independence because they wanted more freedom from England. The Colonies won and the United States of America began!

VOCABULARY EXERCISE
Read these words. Write the words next to their definitions.

a debt   to prevent   to surrender   self-government

an act   to resist   independence   a tax

1. _____ To lose a war or battle and to stop fighting.

2. _____ The money a country owes.

3. _____ A law.

4. _____ Freedom.

5. _____ People pay this money to a government.

6. _____ To fight against something.

7. _____ A government in which the people govern themselves.

8. _____ To stop.

COMPREHENSION EXERCISE.
Answer the questions.

1. Who fought in the French and Indian War?

_____

2. Why do you think the French and Indian War happened?

_____

_____

3. Which taxes did the British create to pay their war debts?

_____

_____

4. Why did the First Continental Congress meet?

_____

_____

5. Why did the Second Continental Congress meet?

_____

_____

6. Who was the leader of the Continental Army?

_____

7. Which battles did Washington lose?

_____

8. Who helped the Colonists?

_____

9. When did the Colonists win the war?

_____

10. When did the English sign the peace treaty?

_____

11. Why do you think it took a long time for England to sign a peace treaty?

_____

_____

GRAMMAR EXERCISE.

```
+-----------------------------------------+
|               PRONOUNS                  |
|                                         |
|  Pronouns refer to people and things.   |
|                                         |
|     Subject  Possessive  Object         |
|       He        his       him           |
|       She       her       her           |
|       It        its       it            |
|       They      their     them          |
+-----------------------------------------+
```

A. Read the passage. Copy three sentences which have a pronoun. Circle the pronoun. Write the word which the pronoun refers to at the end of the sentence.

1. _____

_____

2. _____

_____

3. _____

_____

B. Read the sentences below. Rewrite the sentences using the words the pronouns refer to.

1. They created many new taxes.

_____

2. They were angry.

_____

3. They threw it into the water.

_____

4. The representatives wrote a letter to him.

_____

5. They asked for the rights of self-government.

_____

6. They chose George Washington to be the leader.

_____

7. The delegates wrote it.

_____

8. His soldiers were poorly equipped, but the Colonists defeated them.

_____

9. They won the war.

_____

C. Write four sentences using the pronouns below. Use the information in this lesson.
Write the word which the pronoun refers to at the end of the sentence.

1. he _____

_____

2. it _____

_____

3. they _____

_____

4. them _____

GRAPHICAL LITERACY.
Look at the map and the key. Answer the questions.

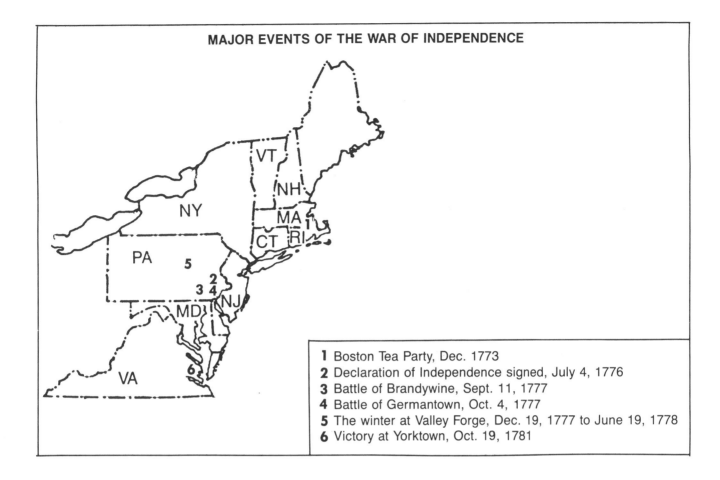

MAJOR EVENTS OF THE WAR OF INDEPENDENCE

1 Boston Tea Party, Dec. 1773
2 Declaration of Independence signed, July 4, 1776
3 Battle of Brandywine, Sept. 11, 1777
4 Battle of Germantown, Oct. 4, 1777
5 The winter at Valley Forge, Dec. 19, 1777 to June 19, 1778
6 Victory at Yorktown, Oct. 19, 1781

1. How many events are listed?

_____

2. When was the Boston Tea Party?

_____

3. When did Washington spend the winter in Valley Forge?

_____

4. In which state is Valley Forge?

_____

5. When did the British surrender at Yorktown?

_____

6. In which state is Yorktown?

_____

WRITING ACTIVITY.
Answer the questions with complete sentences.

1. Identify one law which England made against the colonists.

_____

2. Describe this law.

_____

_____

3. Did the colonists like this law? Why or why not?

_____

_____

4. What did the colonists do?

_____

_____

Use your answers to the above questions to write a paragraph. The title of your paragraph should be: England Makes a Law Against the Colonists.

_____

_____

_____

_____

_____

_____

_____

_____

_____

_____

REVIEW EXERCISE.
Do you remember the meaning of the following words?
Boston Tea Party, First Continental Congress, George Washington, War of Independence, Declaration of Independence

A NATION BEGINS

Discuss these questions with your teacher and class.

1. Who is the President of the U.S.?
2. What does the President do?
3. What is the capital of the U.S.?
4. In which city is the U.S. government?

PRE-READING

In this lesson you will learn about the beginning of the U.S. government. You will also read about the parts of the government that still work today.

CONTENT VOCABULARY
These words are important in this lesson. What do you know about them?

Constitution
Bill of Rights
President of the U.S.
Congress
Supreme Court

SURVEY

Read the subtitles and the words in bold print. Look at the pictures.

1. Which document describes the government?
2. What are the names of the three parts of the government?

Look at the comprehension questions. Try to find the answers to these questions when you read the passage.

A NATION BEGINS

The Continental Congress prepared the **Articles of Confederation.** These Articles were rules to govern the new country. These rules were adopted by the colonies in 1781. Each individual state had a lot of power. The government of the United States was not strong. The government could not establish taxes, and it could not make laws for trade among the states.

Grand Union Flag, America's first official flag
with thirteen stripes for the Thirteen Colonies

The Constitution

united (joined together)

The thirteen states did not form a strong country because the states were not united. George Washington, Alexander Hamilton, James Madison, and other leaders were not satisfied with the government under the Articles of Confederation. There was a meeting in 1787 to change the articles. The delegates at this meeting decided to write a new constitution because they realized that the states needed a strong central government.

The Branches of Government

The new Constitution established three branches of government. They were the **Executive Branch,** the **Judicial Branch,** and the **Legislative Branch.** The President is the head of the Executive Branch. This branch enforces the laws. The people elect the President for a four year term.

population (number of people)

The legislative branch is responsible for making new laws. This branch has two houses — the **Senate** and the **House of Representatives.** They are called the **Congress.** Each state sends two members to the Senate. The House of Representatives is larger than the Senate. The population of a state determines the number of its representatives. The states with more people have more representatives than the states with fewer people.

The Judicial Branch consists of the **Supreme Court** and other Federal courts. This branch is responsible for explaining the Constitution.

George Washington - The First President

The Constitution is Ratified

The delegates signed the Constitution on September 17, 1787. At least nine of the thirteen states had to ratify it. In 1788, nine states ratified the Constitution. By 1790, all states agreed to accept the new Constitution. George Washington was elected the first President in 1789. He became known as the "Father of This Country".

/ratify
(to approve)

The Bill of Rights

The people who wrote the Constitution knew the Constitution was good, but they knew it needed some changes. They established a system for changing the Constitution. This system is known as "amending". The first major changes were ten amendments. They were added in 1791. They are known as the **Bill of Rights.** They guarantee citizens' rights. Some of these rights are the freedom of religion, the freedom of speech, and the right to a trial by jury.

Summary

The Constitution established the government of the United States. The Bill of Rights guaranteed citizens' rights. There have been many changes to the Constitution. These amendments better guarantee the rights of U.S. citizens.

VOCABULARY EXERCISE
Read these words. Write the words next to their definitions.

population   a delegate   united   to ratify   an amendment   to amend

1. _____ To approve something.

2. _____ To change a law.

3. _____ Not separated.

4. _____ People.

5. _____ A change in a law.

6. _____ A person who is chosen to attend a meeting.

COMPREHENSION EXERCISE.
Answer the questions.

1. What were the Articles of Confederation?

_____

_____

2. What are the three branches of the U.S. government?

_____

_____

3. What do the Senate and the House of Representatives do?

_____

4. When did the delegates sign the Constitution?

_____

5. When did all the states ratify the Constitution?

_____

6. Why is amending important?

_____

_____

_____

_____

7. What is the Bill of Rights?

_____

_____

8. What did the Bill of Rights guarantee?

_____

_____

GRAMMAR EXERCISE.

CONJUNCTIONS

AND and **BUT** are conjunctions. They can combine two sentences.
And adds some information. **But** contrasts information.   **Use** a comma before these conjunctions.

Examples:
The Supreme Court explains the laws.
The Supreme Court decides if people are guilty of breaking Federal laws.
The Supreme Court explains the laws, and it decides if people are guilty of breaking Federal laws.

The Constitution was good.
The Constitution needed changes.
The Constitution was good, but it needed changes.

A. Read the passage. Write a sentence with "**and**" and a sentence with "**but**".

1. and _____

_____

2. but _____

_____

B. Read the paragraph below. Complete the sentences by writing either "and" or "but".

The states approved the Articles of Confederation, _____ the government was not

strong. It could not establish taxes, _____ it could not regulate trade. The

delegates wrote a new Constitution. In 1788, nine states ratified the Constitution,

_____ in 1790, all the states agreed to accept it. The Constitution was new,

_____ it soon needed changes. The first changes were the Bill of Rights.

36

C. Combine the sentences. Use "**and**" or "**but**". Use a pronoun in the second part of the sentence.

1. The thirteen states had laws.
   The states did not have a strong government.

   _____

   _____

2. The government could not regulate trade.
   The government could not establish taxes.

   _____

   _____

3. Some representatives realized the states needed a strong central government.
   Some representatives were afraid that the small states would lose power.

   _____

   _____

   _____

   _____

4. George Washington was the first President.
   George Washington became known as the "Father of This Country".

   _____

   _____

   _____

D. Write two sentences. Use the information in this lesson. Combine the sentences using "**and**" or "**but**".

   _____

   _____

   _____

   _____

   _____

   _____

GRAPHICAL LITERACY.
Look at the chart. Answer the questions.

THE U.S. GOVERNMENT TODAY

LEGISLATIVE BRANCH	EXECUTIVE BRANCH	JUDICIAL BRANCH

The Congress

Senate	House of Representatives
100 members elected to a six year term	435 members elected to a two year term
Two per state	Number per state based on population

President and Vice-President

Elected to a four year term

Supreme Court

Nine justices appointed by the President for life

1. What are the three branches of the U.S. government?

_____

_____

2. Who is in the legislative branch?

_____

3. Who is in the executive branch?

_____

4. Who is in the judicial branch?

_____

5. How many senators are in the U.S. Congress? _____

6. How many representatives are in the U.S. Congress? _____

7. How many Supreme Court justices are there? _____

8. How many years is a Senator's term? _____

9. How many years is a Representative's term? _____

10. How many years is the President's term? _____

11. How many years is the Vice-President's term? _____

12. How many years is a Justice's term? _____

WRITING ACTIVITY.
Answer the questions with complete sentences.

1. What happened in 1787?

_____

_____

2. What happened on September 17, 1787?

_____

_____

3. What happened in 1788?

_____

_____

4. What happened in 1790?

_____

_____

Describe how the Constitution was written. Use your answers to the above questions to write a paragraph. The title should be: The Writing of the U.S. Constitution.

_____

_____

_____

_____

_____

_____

_____

_____

_____

REVIEW EXERCISE.
Do you remember the meaning of the following words?
Articles of Confederation, Constitution, President, Congress, Senate, House of Representatives, Supreme Court, Bill Of Rights

UNIT REVIEW
Describe the importance of each person, place, document, or event.

1. Native Americans

_____

_____

2. Jamestown

_____

_____

3. Mayflower Compact

_____

_____

4. First Continental Congress

_____

_____

5. Declaration of Independence

_____

_____

6. The Constitution

_____

_____

7. Bill of Rights

_____

_____

IMPORTANT TIMES
Write the important event that happened in each of these years.

1492 _____

1607 _____

1609 _____

1775-1781 _____

July 4, 1776 _____

1781 _____

1787 _____

1789 _____

UNIT TWO

WESTWARD EXPANSION

THE NORTH AND THE SOUTH

THE CIVIL WAR

THE REUNITED COUNTRY GROWS

WESTWARD EXPANSION

PERSONAL SURVEY
Discuss these questions with your teacher and class.

1. What is the name of your state?
2. Do you know the names of any explorers?
3. Do you know who explored your state?

PRE-READING

The U.S. got new land in the 1800's. The country grew rapidly.
You will read about the new land in this lesson.

CONTENT VOCABULARY
These words are important in this lesson. What do you know about them?

Louisiana Territory
Florida Purchase
Lewis and Clark
Sacagawea
Zebulon Pike

SURVEY
Read the subtitles and the words in bold print. Look at the pictures.

1. Which land did the U.S. buy?

Look at the comprehension questions. Try to find the answers to these questions when you read the passage.

WESTWARD EXPANSION

acquire
(to get)
The United States acquired a lot of land in the early 1800's. Much of this land was bought from other countries. Many men and women explored the new lands.

An explorer in the West

The Louisiana Purchase
France owned land west of the Mississippi River. This land was called the **Louisiana Territory.** France's leader, Napoleon Bonaparte, was fighting a war in Europe. He needed money to fight the war. Therefore, he sold the Louisiana Territory to the United States in 1803. **President Thomas Jefferson** paid fifteen million dollars for the land. This purchase was very important because it almost doubled the size of the United States.

People Explore the Louisiana Territory
Thomas Jefferson wanted to explore the Louisiana Territory. In 1804, he sent **Meriwether Lewis** and **William Clark** to the territory. They traveled on the Mississippi River and westward to the beginning of the Missouri River. An Indian woman named **Sacagawea** was their guide. They explored the present states of North Dakota and Montana. They also explored areas as far west as the **Oregon Territory.**

In 1805, **Zebulon Pike** headed west into the new Louisiana Territory. He followed the upper Arkansas River to the Rocky Mountains. He went as far as the present state of
discover Colorado. He discovered a large mountain. In fact, it is known today as Pike's Peak.
(to find)

The Florida Purchase
In 1800, Spain still owned a large territory in North America. It was in the present state of Florida. In 1819, the United States got this territory from Spain. This was called the Florida Purchase. Now the United States owned much of the land from the Atlantic Ocean to the Rocky Mountains. Texas, however, was a part of Mexico.

Summary
The United States expanded rapidly during the 1800's. It owned all the land between the Atlantic Ocean and the Rocky Mountains except for Texas.

AN IMPORTANT PERSON IN U.S. HISTORY: Sacagawea

A statue of Sacagawea at the Buffalo Bill Historical Center
SACAGAWEA 10' at Cody, WY, USA © Harry Jackson 1980 Photo by Ed Leikam © WFS, Inc. 1980.

Sacagawea was a Indian woman. She belonged to the Shoshoni tribe. Her name means "Bird Woman". She was born in Idaho about 1787. Sacagawea was captured by enemy Indians when she was about fourteen years old. She was sold as a slave to a French trader. His name was Charbonneau. Later she married him. In 1804, Lewis and Clark hired Charbonneau as a guide. Sacagawea and their baby son came with them. Charbonneau began to lead the expedition west.

Sacagawea knew the Shoshoni territory very well. Therefore, Sacagawea became the guide when the expedition reached the Shoshoni Territory. In the present state of Montana, Sacagawea met her own Shoshoni tribe. The Shoshonis gave the expedition food and horses. They helped the explorers to reach the Pacific Coast. Sacagawea led the party back to Missouri. Lewis and Clark paid Sacagawea and Charbonneau for their help. Sacagawea was very important to Lewis and Clark. In fact, Lewis and Clark mentioned Sacagawea and her son, Jean-Baptiste, almost daily in a journal which they wrote.

Some people believe that Sacagawea died very young. However, in 1875, a missionary found an old Shoshoni woman who said she was Sacagawea. This Shoshoni woman died in 1884 when she was almost 100 years old.

Few people knew anything about Sacagawea for over 100 years after the expedition. However, most people today recognize that Sacagawea helped the Lewis and Clark expedition. There are many monuments named for Sacagawea. In fact, there are even a river and mountain pass named for her!

VOCABULARY EXERCISE
Read these words. Write the words next to their definitions.

a territory   a guide   explore   an expedition
acquire   discover

1. _____ A person who leads people into a new land.

2. _____ To get something.

3. _____ An area of land before it becomes a state.

4. _____ To travel through a new land and make maps.

5. _____ A group of people who are exploring

6. _____ To find for the first time.

COMPREHENSION EXERCISE.
Answer the questions.

1. Why did France sell the Louisiana Territory to the U.S.? _____

_____

_____

2. Why was the Louisiana Territory important? _____

_____

3. How did the U.S. get Florida? _____

_____

4. Who explored the Louisiana Territory? _____

_____

5. How did the Shoshonis help Lewis and Clark? _____

_____

6. What area did Zebulon Pike explore? _____

_____

7. Was Sacagawea important to the exploration of the Louisiana Territory? Why or why not?

_____

_____

GRAMMAR EXERCISE.

CONNECTING WORDS join ideas. They can introduce sentences.

However contrasts ideas.
Example: The trip was hard. However, it was a success.

In fact provides more information.
Example: The trip was hard. In fact, it took many years.

Therefore explains a result.
Example: The trip was hard. Therefore, the explorers rested a long time.

A. Read the passage. Find sentences with "however", "in fact", and "therefore". Copy a sentence with each connector below.

1. however _____

_____

2. in fact _____

_____

3. therefore _____

_____

B. Write the correct connector. Use either "however", "in fact", or "therefore".

1. President Jefferson bought the Louisiana Territory. He did not know much about the land.

_____, he sent explorers.

2. The expedition traveled many miles. _____, the trip lasted two years.

3. Some people believe that Sacagawea died very young. _____,

in 1875, a missionary found an old Shoshoni woman who said she was Sacagawea.

48

C. Complete the sentences below.

1. Sacagawea married Charbonneau. Therefore, _____

_____

_____

2. Sacagawea had a new baby son. Therefore, _____

_____

_____

3. Charbonneau began as the guide. Soon, however, _____

_____

_____

4. Sacagawea was very important to the expedition. In fact, _____

_____

_____

5. Many people think that Sacagawea lived a long time. In fact, _____

_____

_____

6. Sacagawea was famous. Therefore, _____

_____

_____

D. Write a sentence for each connector. Use the information from the lesson. Remember the sentences must be true!

1. in fact _____

_____

2. however _____

_____

3. therefore _____

_____

GRAPHICAL LITERACY.
Look at the map. Answer the questions.

LEWIS AND CLARK EXPEDITION

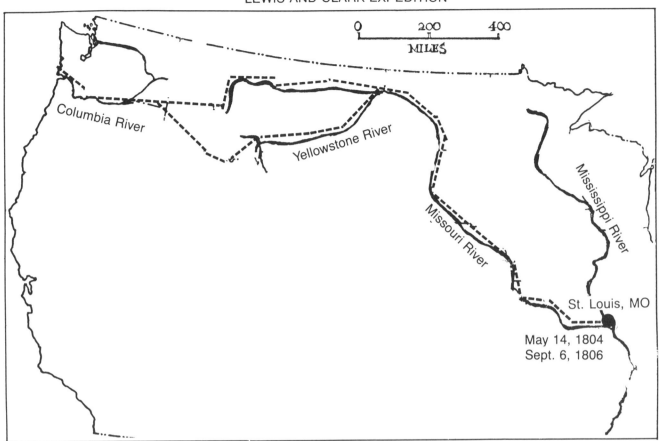

1. Where did Lewis and Clark begin their trip? _____

   _____

2. Which states did Lewis and Clark explore? _____

   _____

3. Which rivers did they use? _____

   _____

4. How far west did they go? _____

   _____

5. How long were they gone? _____

   _____

6. Where did they end their trip? _____

   _____

WRITING ACTIVITY

Pretend you are the explorer William Clark. Write a short letter to your family. Describe what you are seeing in the territory. The questions below can help you.

What does the land look like?
How are you traveling?
What kinds of animals do you see?
What do you eat?
Where do you sleep?
Do you see any other people?

May 18, 1805

Dear _____,

_____

_____

_____

_____

_____

_____

_____

_____

_____

_____

_____

_____

_____

_____

_____

_____

_____

_____

REVIEW EXERCISE.
Do you remember the meaning of the following words?
Louisiana Territory, Meriwether Lewis, William Clark, Sacagawea, Zebulon Pike, Florida Purchase

THE NORTH AND THE SOUTH

PERSONAL SURVEY
Discuss these questions with your teacher and class.

1. Which states have you visited or lived in?
2. What are some states in the northeastern part of the U.S.?
3. What are some states in the southeastern part of the U.S.?
4. How are the northeastern states different from the southeastern states?

PRE-READING

The North and South were very different from each other in the 1800's. These differences caused many problems. You will read about their differences in this lesson.

CONTENT VOCABULARY
These words are important in this lesson. What do you know about them?

the North
the South
slavery

SURVEY
Read the subtitles and the words in bold print. Look at the pictures.

1. What was an important difference between the North and the South?

Look at the comprehension questions. Try to find the answers to these questions when you read the passage.

THE NORTH AND THE SOUTH

In the 1800's, the northern and southern parts of the United States started to have problems. The northern and southern parts are shown on the map.

A factory in the North   A slave picking cotton

Differences Between the North and the South

The North and South had many differences. They had different climates, economies, and attitudes. The North had colder weather than the South. This weather affected the economy. The North was involved in fishing and trading. The North had small farms which grew corn and wheat. Farmers raised livestock and sheep for wool. The North also began to develop many textile factories.

textile (cloth)

In the South, the climate was warmer. The climate was better for farming. The South grew such crops as tobacco, cotton, rice, and sugar. Southern farms were larger than northern farms. The large southern farms were called plantations. These **plantations** needed many workers to plant and harvest the crops. The plantation owners wanted good, cheap labor. Therefore, they used **slaves.** The South exported its crops to the North and to other countries. Manufacturing was more important to the North than to the South. There were few factories in the South. The South imported manufactured products from the North and from other countries.

The North Opposes Slavery

oppose (to fight against something)

The first Blacks arrived in the Colonies in 1619. First, they helped to grow tobacco in the South. Not everyone liked slavery. George Washington, the first President, did not like slavery, but he did not stop it. Congress made a law in 1808. This law prohibited new slaves from entering the United States. However, people began to smuggle new slaves from other countries into the United States.

Congress Passes Tariffs

The U.S. government wanted to protect its manufactured and farm products. In 1816 and also in 1828, Congress passed protective **tariffs.** A tariff is a tax on products brought into a country. There were tariffs on wool and manufactured products brought into the U.S.

Because of these tariffs, imported products became more expensive than products made in the U.S. The South was unhappy because Southerners needed these products and they had to pay more money for them. One time, South Carolina, refused to pay the tariff. Later, they paid it. However, this was the first time a state refused to obey a law of the United States!

Do New States Become Slave States or Free States?

Both the North and the South wanted power in Congress. In 1820, two new states wanted to become a part of the United States. These states were Maine in the North and Missouri in the West. The North and the South made an agreement called the **Missouri Compromise.** Missouri entered as a slave state and Maine entered as a Free state. This Compromise also prohibited slavery in all new states north of Missouri's southern border.

The slavery debate continued in the 1830's and 1840's. In 1848, the United States acquired new territory fom Mexico. People asked the question: Would the new states be free states or slave states? California became a free state in 1848. The **Compromise of 1850** allowed the people in the new territory to vote. They decided if they wanted to become a free state or a slave state. The Compromise of 1850 established the **Fugitive Slave Act.** Many slaves escaped from the South and went North. This law said that the North should return those slaves.

Opposition to Slavery Continues

In 1857, the U.S. Supreme Court made the **Dred Scott Decision.** This decision declared the Missouri Compromise unconstitutional. It said that Congress could not prohibit slavery in a state, however, a state could prohibit slavery within its borders. This decision angered the North. Many Northerners wrote angry articles in the newspapers. They continued to talk about ending slavery.

Summary

There were many differences between the North and the South. The North and South had many problems. They tried to solve their problems through compromises. Soon, they could not make any more compromises and the Civil War would begin.

VOCABULARY EXERCISE
Read these words. Write the words next to their definitions.

to export   a plantation   a tariff   unconstitutional

to import   climate   to oppose   a compromise

1. _____ To be against.

2. _____ A large farm in the South.

3. _____ A tax on imported products.

4. _____ To sell products to another country.

5. _____ To buy products from another country.

6. _____ The weather.

7. _____ A law or rule which is not in agreement with the U.S. Constitution.

8. _____ An agreement.

COMPREHENSION EXERCISE.
Answer the questions.

1. Describe the economy of the North.

_____

_____

2. Describe the economy of the South.

_____

_____

3. Why did the South use slaves?

_____

_____

4. What is a tariff?

_____

_____

_____

5. Why do you think Congress passed the tariffs?

_____

_____

_____

6. What did the Missouri Compromise do?

_____

_____

_____

7. Do you think the North and the South wanted a Civil War? Why or why not?

_____

_____

_____

GRAMMAR EXERCISE.

COMPARATIVE ADJECTIVES

Add "er" to one syllable adjectives or two syllable adjectives which end in "y". Then use "than".
Example: The Southern farms were bigger than the Northern farms.

Use "more" before adjectives with two or more syllables.
Example: Imported products are more expensive than American products.

REMEMBER these irregular forms: good-better and bad-worse.

A. Read the passage. Copy two comparative sentences. One should have "adjective + er" and the other "more + adjective".

1._____

_____

_____

2._____

_____

_____

56

B. Write a sentence for each comparison below.

1. Compare a northern farm with a southern farm. Use the word "large".

_____

_____

2. Compare the climate in the North with the climate in the South. Use the word "cold".

_____

_____

3. Compare the weather in the South with the weather in the North. Use the word "warm".

_____

_____

4. Compare the prices of imported products with the prices of American products. Use the word "high".

_____

_____

5. Compare imported farm products with American farm products. Use the word "expensive".

_____

_____

6. Compare American manufactured products with imported manufactured products. Use the word "cheap".

_____

_____

C. Write two sentences which make comparisons. Use the information from this lesson. Remember the sentences must be true!

1. _____

_____

2. _____

_____

GRAPHICAL LITERACY.
Look at the charts. Answer the questions.

THE NORTH AND THE SOUTH IN 1860

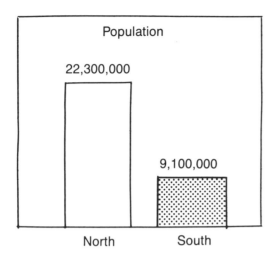

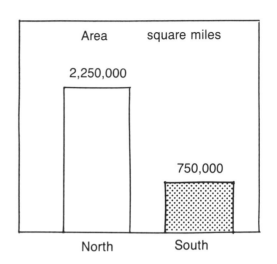

1. In 1860, what was the population of the North?

_____

2. In 1860, what was the population of the South?

_____

3. Did the North or the South have more people?

_____

4. How many more people did the North have?

_____

5. How large was the North?

_____

6. How large was the South?

_____

7. Was the South larger than the North?

_____

8. How much larger was the North?

_____

WRITING ACTIVITY.
Answer the questions with complete sentences.

1. What are some states in the North?

_____

2. Describe the weather, the economy, and the farms in the North.

_____

_____

3. What are some states in the South?

_____

4. Describe the weather, the economy, and the farms in the South.

_____

_____

Write one paragraph describing the North and another paragraph describing the South. Use your answers to the above questions. The title should be: The North and the South.

_____

_____

_____

_____

_____

_____

_____

_____

_____

_____

_____

REVIEW EXERCISE.
Do you remember the meaning of the following words?
Plantations, slaves, tariffs, Missouri Compromise, Compromise of 1850, Dred Scott Decision

THE CIVIL WAR

PERSONAL SURVEY
Discuss these questions with your teacher and class.

1. A war between people in the same country is called a civil war. Why do you think people fight a civil war?
2. Why is civil war difficult for the people in the country?
3. Do you know about any civil wars?
4. Does anyone really win a civil war?

PRE-READING

The differences between the North and the South resulted in a war. This was called the Civil War. You will read about the Civil War in this lesson.

CONTENT VOCABULARY
These words are important in this lesson. What do you know about them?

the Union
the Confederacy
Abraham Lincoln
Jefferson Davis
Ulysses S. Grant

SURVEY

Read the subtitles and the words in bold print. Look at the pictures.

1. Who was the U.S. President during the Civil War?
2. Where was the Civil War?
3. Who won the Civil War?

Look at the comprehension questions. Try to find the answers to these questions when you read the passage.

THE CIVIL WAR

The North and South had many differences. They made many compromises to solve their problems. Soon, they could not find solutions to their problems.

The First States Secede

secede (to leave the Union)

Abraham Lincoln was elected President in 1860. Soon after this election, South Carolina seceded from the U.S. Soon, Georgia, Texas and other states also left. The South established its own government. The South called itself the **Confederate States of America.** The capital was in Richmond, Virginia. The South elected **Jefferson Davis** as its President. Robert E. Lee was the general of the army.

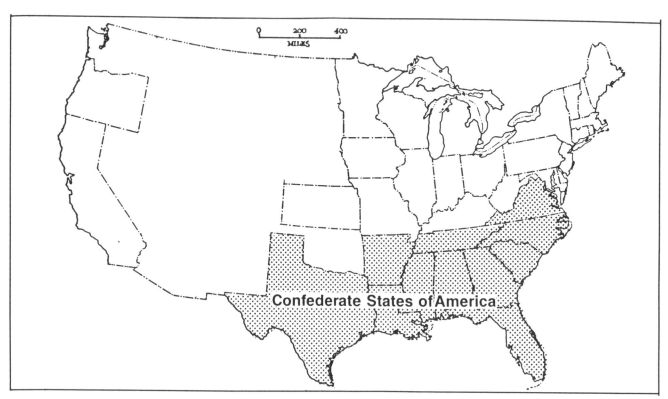

The North and the South

The Civil War Begins

On April 12, 1861, the South attacked **Fort Sumter** in South Carolina. Fort Sumter belonged to the North. President Lincoln did not want a civil war, but now he had no choice. The **Confederacy** (the South) and the **Union** (the North) were at war.

The War At Sea

Both the Confederacy and the Union had navies. The Union Navy tried to prevent the Confederacy from sending its cotton to other countries. It blocked the Confederate ports. The Confederacy tried to break this blockade. It sent a warship called the **Merrimack** to attack the Union ships. The Merrimack had iron plates to protect it. At this time, all other ships were made of wood. The Union was ready for the Merrimack. The Union had a ship called the **Monitor.** It also had iron. The two ships fought, but neither won the battle. The battle between the Monitor and the Merrimack did not end the war. However, navies around the world started to build ships with iron plates.

61

The War On Land

In 1864, the Union developed a plan to win the war. **General, Ulysses S. Grant,** fought his way from the North to Richmond, Virginia. At the same time, **General William T. Sherman** fought his way from the North through the South. He finally reached Savannah, Georgia which is on the Atlantic Ocean. He had cut the Confederacy in half! His march to the sea was very destructive. He destroyed everything of value. He destroyed both cities and plantations.

Ruins in Richmond, VA, May 1865

The Confederacy Surrenders

The Confederacy was losing the war. Finally, on April 9, 1865, General Lee surrendered to General Grant at the **Appomattox Court House** in Virginia. General Sherman continued to fight in the South. Soon after, the remaining Confederate armies surrendered to him. The long Civil War of the United States had come to an end. It had lasted from 1861 to 1865.

Summary

The North and the South fought the Civil War because of slavery and other problems. The North finally won the war. Both the North and the South lost many people. The United States had to rebuild itself after this very destructive war.

VOCABULARY EXERCISE

A. Read the nouns below. Find the verbs in the reading passage. Write them below.

NOUN	VERB
destruction	_____
secession	_____
election	_____
solution	_____

B. Write the correct form of the above words in the sentences. Remember to use the correct noun form or the correct verb tense!

1. The southern states _____ from the U.S.

2. The North and the South could not _____ their problems.

3. General Sherman's march to the sea caused a lot of _____ in the South.

4. The North _____ Lincoln President and the South

   _____ Davis President.

COMPREHENSION EXERCISE.
Answer the questions.

1. When did the Southern states begin to secede?

_____

_____

2. What were the names of the two sides of the Civil War?

_____

_____

3. Did President Lincoln want a civil war?

_____

4. Name an important general for the Union and an important general for the Confederacy.

_____

_____

63

5. What was General Sherman's plan to win?

_____

_____

6. Did the North really win the Civil War? Why or why not?

_____

_____

_____

_____

_____

GRAMMAR EXERCISE.

```
┌─────────────────────────────────────────┐
│              PRONOUNS                     │
│  Pronouns refer to people and things.     │
│                                           │
│        Subject Possessive Object          │
│          He       his       him           │
│          She      her       her           │
│          It       its       it            │
│          They     their     them          │
└─────────────────────────────────────────┘
```

A. Read the passage. Find a sentence with "it", "its", "him", and "their". Copy the sentences below. Write the names of the people or things they refer to at the end of the sentences.

1. it _____

_____

2. its _____

_____

3. him _____

_____

4. their _____

_____

B. Rewrite the sentences using the words the pronouns refer to.

1. Plantation owners used <u>them</u> as workers.

_____

2. <u>It</u> did not support slavery.

_____

3. <u>They</u> seceded from the United States.

_____

4. The South attacked <u>it</u> on April 12, 1861.

_____

5. <u>They</u> had navies.

_____

6. <u>He</u> was from Virginia.

_____

7. <u>It</u> was called the Monitor.

_____

8. <u>He</u> destroyed everything of value on his way to Savannah.

_____

9. <u>It</u> surrendered in 1865.

_____

10. <u>It</u> began in 1861 and ended in 1865.

_____

C. Write sentences. Use the pronouns ''it'', ''its'', and ''they''. Write the words they refer to at the end of the sentences. Use the information from this lesson.

1. it _____

_____

2. its _____

_____

3. they _____

_____

GRAPHICAL LITERACY.
Look at the map and the key. Answer the questions.

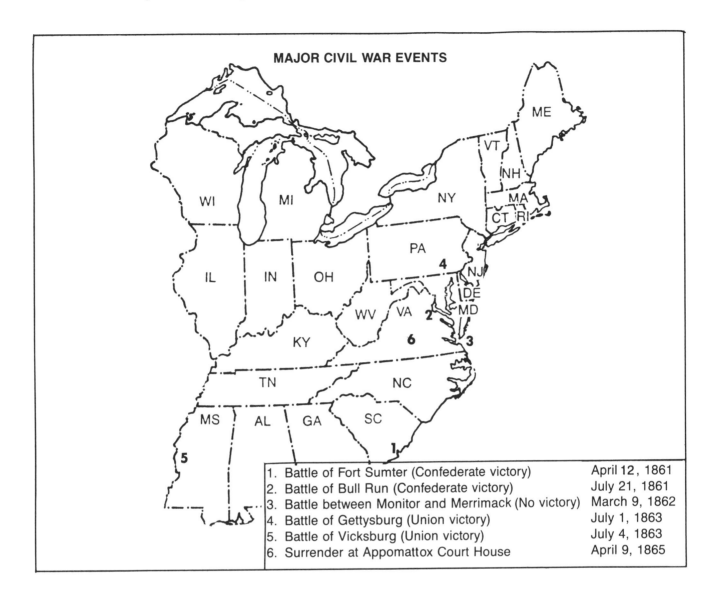

MAJOR CIVIL WAR EVENTS

1. Battle of Fort Sumter (Confederate victory)   April 12, 1861
2. Battle of Bull Run (Confederate victory)   July 21, 1861
3. Battle between Monitor and Merrimack (No victory)   March 9, 1862
4. Battle of Gettysburg (Union victory)   July 1, 1863
5. Battle of Vicksburg (Union victory)   July 4, 1863
6. Surrender at Appomattox Court House   April 9, 1865

1. How many battles are listed on the key? _____

2. When was the Battle of Fort Sumter? _____

3. When was the Battle of Bull Run? _____

4. When was the Battle between the Monitor and the Merrimack? _____

5. When did the Confederacy surrender? _____

6. In what state was the Battle of Fort Sumter? _____

7. In what state was the Battle of Gettysburg? _____

8. Where is the Appomattox Court House? _____

WRITING EXERCISE.
Answer the questions with complete sentences.

1. Identify three events that helped the North to end the war.

_____

_____

_____

2. Explain how each helped the North to win the war.

_____

_____

_____

_____

Describe why the North won the Civil War. Use your answers to write a paragraph. The title should be: Why the North Won the Civil War.

_____

_____

_____

_____

_____

_____

_____

_____

_____

_____

_____

_____

REVIEW EXERCISE.
Do you remember the meaning of the following words?
Civil War, Abraham Lincoln, Jefferson Davis, Union, Confederacy, Appomatox Court House

THE REUNITED COUNTRY GROWS

PERSONAL SURVEY
Discuss these questions with your teacher and class.

1. When a civil war ends, what do the people have to do?
2. What changes do people make after a civil war?
3. What changes does a government make after a civil war?

PRE-READING

The U.S. had to rebuild the South after the Civil War. During this time, the U.S. also expanded into the West. You will read about the rapid growth of the U.S. in the late 1800's in this lesson.

CONTENT VOCABULARY
These words are important in this lesson. What do you know about them?

Fourteenth Amendment
Reconstruction
Alaska
Pony Express
reservations for the Native Americans

SURVEY
Read the subtitles and the words in bold print. Look at the pictures.

1. What happened to the South?
2. Where did the U.S. expand?

Look at the comprehension questions. Try to find the answers to these questions when you read the passage.

THE REUNITED COUNTRY GROWS

The North won the Civil War. The North did not want slavery. After the war, Congress passed the **Fourteenth Amendment.** This Amendment gave citizenship to all former slaves. They were called **freedmen.**

The South Is Rebuilt

in ruins (destroyed)

After the war, the South was in ruins. Many battles had been fought in the South. Many cities and farms had been destroyed. Many people lost everything they owned. People could not find work. Some people in the North wanted to punish the South. The U.S. army occupied the South. Congress passed the Fourteenth Amendment. It guaranteed rights to all citizens. If a Confederate state did not accept the amendment, it could not re-enter the U.S.

lumber (wood)

The time after the Civil War was called **Reconstruction.** It took more than ten years for the South to rebuild itself. A new economic system developed in the South. Slavery was not legal. Plantations were divided into tenant farms. People either rented the land, or they farmed the land and gave a part of their crops to the land owners. Industry began to develop in major Southern cities like Birmingham, Alabama. The lumber and textile industries also expanded in the South during this time. The whole nation, North and South, was growing rapidly.

Wagon train going West

The U.S. Expands to the West

Many people moved westward. First, gold was discovered in California, Colorado, and South Dakota. Silver was also discovered in Nevada. Many people went West to look for gold and silver. They wanted to become rich. Second, the **Homestead Act of 1862** offered free land to people who settled in the West. This was a good opportunity for people to get their own land. When a territory had enough people, it could vote to become a state. There were three new states in the West during and soon after the Civil War: Nevada in 1864, Nebraska in 1867, and Colorado in 1876.

In 1867, the Secretary of State William Seward wanted to buy **Alaska** from Russia. He convinced Congress to pay $7,200,000 for Alaska. At the time, many people did not want to buy Alaska. They called Alaska "Seward's Folly." Later, people would realize that Alaska was very important.

A stagecoach

Two Major Events Unite the East and the West

Before 1858, transportation was not good. Mail did not travel fast in the U.S. In 1858, the Southerland Overland Mail Company began a stagecoach line. It offered mail service from Missouri to California. In 1860, the **Pony Express** began to carry mail from Missouri to California. They used a series of "relay" riders who passed the mail from one horse rider to another. In 1861, a telegraph line connected New York with San Francisco.

The railroad also helped to unite the East with the West. In 1862, Congress asked the Union Pacific Railroad and the Central Pacific Railroad to build a railroad which would join the East and the West. The Union Pacific Railroad started its railroad in Iowa and built it towards the West. The Central Pacific Railroad started its railroad in California and built it towards the East. The railroads met at **Promontory Point, Utah** in 1869. The final rail link between the East and the West was made!

Native Americans

A sad part of American history involved the Native Americans. Many of the hundreds of tribes throughout North America lived off the land. They hunted, fished, and grew food. As the settlers moved into the new lands in the West, the Indians were forced to move. The settlers pushed the Native Americans farther and farther from their lands. In fact, most Eastern tribes were pushed west of the Mississippi River by the middle of the 1800's. There were not many places the Native Americans could go.

There were many battles between the settlers and the Native Americans. Many times the U.S. Army fought the Native Americans. After the Army won these battles, the government established **reservations** for the Native Americans. A reservation was land which the government reserved for Native Americans. The government established reservations in many parts of the U.S. Often the land was not good. Life was very hard. In many cases, the government sent different tribes to live on the same reservation. This is not a proud part of U.S. history.

Summary

The U.S. grew rapidly after the Civil War. The South rebuilt itself over the next ten years. The U.S. expanded westward rapidly. Native Americans became the victims of the westward move. Railroads provided transportation and communication between the East and the West.

VOCABULARY EXERCISE
Read these words. Write the correct words in the sentences.

lumber   relay   a reservation
textile   to reserve   freedmen

1. _____ were slaves who were received their freedom after the Civil War.

2. The _____ industry prepares wood for sale.

3. The U.S. government _____ land for the Native Americans.

4. The _____ industry makes cloth.

5. The U.S. government sent the Native Americans to _____ after the U.S. army defeated them.

6. A _____ rider carried the mail on horseback and gave it to another rider.

COMPREHENSION EXERCISE.
Answer the questions.

1. What did the Fourteenth Amendment do?

_____

_____

_____

2. What was the time after the Civil War called?

_____

3. How did the South's economy change after the war?

_____

_____

_____

4. How did the Homestead Act of 1862 help to expand the U.S.?

_____

_____

_____

5. What are three ways communication improved in the U.S.?

_____

_____

_____

6. Why is Promontory Point important?

_____

_____

7. What happened to the Native Americans when the settlers moved West?

_____

_____

8. Was the U.S. government right or wrong when it made reservations for the Native Americans?

_____

_____

_____

GRAMMAR EXERCISE.

```
NEGATIVE PAST TENSE

Use NOT after the verb "be" and after "could".
Examples: were - were not and could - could not

Use DID NOT before all other verbs. Remember to change the verb form!
Examples: live - did not live and came - did not come
```

A. Read the passage. Find two sentences that use the negative past tense form. Copy them below.

1. _____

_____

2. _____

_____

B. Read the verbs below. Change them to the positive, past tense and the negative, past tense.

	POSITIVE PAST TENSE	NEGATIVE PAST TENSE
1. begin		
2. buy		
3. connect		
4. can		
5. expand		
6. rebuild		
7. send		
8. want		
9. is		
10. are		

C. Read the sentences below. Complete the sentences by writing either the positive, past tense or the negative, past tense of a verb. Use the verbs below.

begin   buy   connect   can   expand   rebuild   send   want   is   are

1. The South _____ in ruins after the war.

2. Many Black freedmen _____ find work after the war.

3. Industry _____ in the South.

4. The South _____ itself during the ten years after the Civil War.

5. In 1869, the railroads _____ the East with the West.

6. The Pony Express _____ to carry mail from Missouri to California in 1860.

7. The U.S. _____ Alaska for more than seven million dollars.

8. Alaska _____ a bad purchase.

9. The U.S. _____ the Native Americans to reservations.

10. The Native Americans _____ to lose their lands.

D. Write two sentences in the positive, past tense and two sentences in the negative, past tense. Use the information in this lesson.

1. _____

2. _____

73

GRAPHICAL LITERACY.
Look at the chart. Answer the questions.

SOLDIERS KILLED IN THE CIVIL WAR

NORTH ■■■■■■■■■
　　　　■■■■■■■■

SOUTH ☐☐☐☐☐☐☐☐☐
　　　　☐☐☐

Each symbol represents 20,000 men.

---

1. How many men does each square represent? _____

2. Do the white squares represent the North or the South?

_____

3. Do the black squares represent the North or the South?

_____

4. How many Union soldiers died? _____

5. How many Confederate soldiers died? _____

6. What is the total number of soldiers who died? _____

7. Did the North or the South lose more soldiers? _____

WRITING ACTIVITY.
Pretend you are one of the following:
Jim Smith, a soldier in the Union army
Dennis Jones, a soldier in the Confederate army
Ann Jefferson, a housewife in Georgia
Daniel Washington, a freed slave
Mary Johnson, a freed slave

Write a letter to a friend. Explain how the Civil War changed your life.

Sept. 2, 1865

Dear _____,

_____

_____

_____

_____

_____

_____

_____

_____

_____

_____

_____

_____

_____

_____

_____

_____

Sincerely,

_____

REVIEW EXERCISE.
Do you remember the meaning of the following words?
Reconstruction, Fourteenth Amendment, Homestead Act of 1862, Alaska, Pony Express, Native American reservations

UNIT REVIEW
Describe the importance of each person, place, document, or event.

1. Louisiana Territory

_____

_____

2. the Civil War

_____

_____

3. the North

_____

_____

4. the Confederate States of America

_____

_____

5. Abraham Lincoln

_____

_____

6. Robert E. Lee

_____

_____

7. the Fourteenth Amendment

_____

_____

IMPORTANT TIMES
Write the important event that happened in each of these years.

1803 _____

1860 _____

April 12, 1861 _____

April 9, 1865 _____

1861-1865 _____

1867 _____

UNIT THREE

INDUSTRIAL EXPANSION

EARLY IMMIGRATION

WORLD WAR I

GOOD TIMES AND BAD TIMES

INDUSTRIAL EXPANSION

PERSONAL SURVEY
Discuss these questions with your teacher and class.

1. What would your life be like without electricity? Without a telephone? Without a car?
2. Do you know anyone who belongs to a union? What does a union do?

PRE-READING

During the late 1800's, industry and manufacturing began to expand in the U.S. and in other parts of the world. Many inventions helped this industrial expansion. These inventions also changed life in the entire world. In this lesson, you will read about these inventions, the development of big business, and the beginning of unions.

CONTENT VOCABULARY
These words are important in this lesson. What do you know about them?

Thomas Alva Edison
Alexander Graham Bell
Wilbur and Orville Wright
Andrew Carnegie
John D. Rockefeller

SURVEY
Read the first paragraph, the subtitles, the words in bold print, and the summary. Look at the pictures.

1. Which Americans made important inventions?
2. How did industry change?

Look at the comprehension questions. Try to find the answers to these questions when you read the passage.

INDUSTRIAL EXPANSION

In the late 1800's, industry began to expand throughout the entire world. The U.S. was a major leader in industrial expansion.

Flight of the Wright Brothers at Kitty Hawk, NC. Dec. 17, 1903

Americans Make Many Inventions

invention (a new product)

There were many inventions in the U.S. **Thomas Edison** invented the electric light in 1879. In 1876, **Alexander Graham Bell** invented the telephone. At first, people did not take Bell's invention seriously. Soon, people realized that the telephone was very important for communication.

In 1892, the Duryea brothers made the first successful gasoline automobile. Henry Ford and other people built factories to make automobiles. The invention of the gasoline engine also helped the invention of the airplane. On December 17, 1903, **Wilbur and Orville Wright** made the first successful flight in an airplane. They flew 120 feet (37 meters) in 12 seconds!

Big Business Begins

During the early days of industrial expansion, some people became rich and powerful. Two of these people were **Andrew Carnegie** and **John D. Rockefeller.** Andrew Carnegie was in the steel industry. He bought many different companies. First, he bought ships to carry iron from the Great Lakes. Then, he bought railroads and coal mines. He created the largest steel company at this time. Carnegie was the most important person in the steel industry.

lease (to rent)

John D. Rockefeller began his business in oil. He made gasoline by refining oil. Then, he leased land. He also drilled oil wells. He bought railroads and pipelines to transport the oil. His company was the beginning of the Standard Oil Company. John D. Rockefeller became the richest man in the oil business.

Workers Organize

The big companies needed many laborers. These laborers worked hard for many hours. The laborers began to organize **unions.** The unions helped to get better salaries, benefits, and working conditions for the workers. The first major union was the Knights of Labor in 1869. Another union was the American Federation of Labor which is still an important union today.

laborer (a worker)

Summary

There were many inventions in the U.S. during the late 1800's and early 1900's. Industry expanded greatly for many years. The labor force organized unions. The U.S. became a world leader at this time.

AN IMPORTANT PERSON: Thomas Alva Edison

Thomas Alva Edison was born in 1847. His great-grandfather had come to the U.S. from the Netherlands. Edison had a difficult childhood. He went to school for only three months. Then, his mother tutored him in reading at home. Edison became sick. He had scarlet fever. He became partially deaf because of his illness. He had difficulty hearing.

When Edison was ten years old, he became very interested in science, especially chemistry. Edison made many experiments. He needed money for the experiments. He sold fruit, candy, and newspapers on trains. He set up a small, secret laboratory on a train. He did experiments with chemicals and batteries there.

In 1877, Edison invented the first phonograph. It played records. He made many inventions including the electric light bulb, the motion picture machine, and a storage battery. Because of his many inventions, people call him "the greatest American inventor".

VOCABULARY EXERCISE.
Read these words. Write the words next to their definitions.

an invention   to refine   a laborer   a phonograph   a union   to transport

1. _____ A new machine or product.

2. _____ To make gasoline from oil.

3. _____ A labor organization.

4. _____ To carry something from one place to another.

5. _____ A record player.

6. _____ A worker.

COMPREHENSION EXERCISE.
Answer the questions.

1. What were three inventions of the 1800's?

_____

_____

2. What invention helped the development of the automobile and airplane?

_____

3. How did Carnegie and Rockefeller create their big businesses?

_____

_____

_____

4. Why did workers join unions?

_____

_____

5. Do you think the big business owners liked the unions? Why or why not?

_____

_____

_____

_____

GRAMMAR EXERCISE.

TIME PHRASES

In indicates a specific point in time.
Examples: In 1986, in the morning, in the 1800's.

On indicates specific days and dates.
Examples: On Saturday, on July 4th.

For indicates a quantity of time.
Examples: For ten years, for many years.

During indicates a period of time.
Examples: During the 1800's, during the year.
NOTE: If the time phrase comes at the beginning of the sentence, use a comma after it.
EXAMPLE: The Wright brothers invented the airplane in 1903.
In 1903, the Wright brothers invented the airplane.

A. Read the passage. Find sentences which contain a time phrase with ''in'', ''on'', ''for'', and ''during''. Copy the sentences below.

1. in _____

_____

2. on _____

_____

3. for _____

_____

4. during _____

_____

B. Complete the sentences by writing ''in'', ''on'', ''for'', or ''during''.

1. There were many inventions _____ the 1800's and early 1900's.

2. _____ 1876, Alexander Graham Bell invented the telephone.

3. _____ 1879, Thomas Edison invented the electric light.

4. _____ December 17, 1903, the Wright Brothers made the first airplane flight.

5. These inventions helped industry to expand rapidly _____ many years.

C. Write two sentences with time phrases. Use the information from this lesson.

1. _____

2. _____

GRAMMAR EXERCISE.

SUPERLATIVE ADJECTIVES

Add "the" before the adjective. Add "est" to all one syllable and some two syllable adjectives.
Example: The Wright Brothers' plane flew the longest distance.

Use "the most" before adjectives with two or more syllables.
Example: Edison was the most important inventor of the 1800's.

REMEMBER these irregular forms: good—the best and bad—the worst.

A. Read the passage. Find a sentence with the "adjective + est" and another sentence with "the most + adjective".

1. _____

_____

2. _____

_____

B. Write the correct form of the adjective.

1. There were many inventors but Edison was _____ American inventor. (great)

2. There were a few unions in the U.S., but _____ union was the Knights of Labor. (important)

3. The Standard Oil Company became _____ oil company. (large)

4. Carnegie was _____ steel businessman in the U.S. (powerful)

C. Write two sentences which make a comparison. Use the information from this lesson.

1. _____

_____

2. _____

_____

85

GRAPHICAL LITERACY.
Look at the charts. Answer the questions.

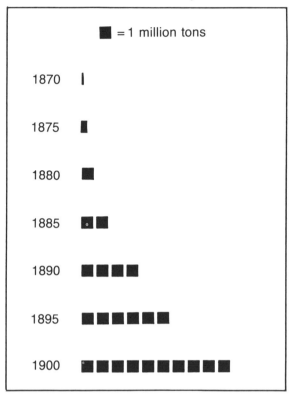

U.S. STEEL PRODUCTION, 1870-1900

■ = 1 million tons

1870
1875
1880
1885
1890
1895
1900

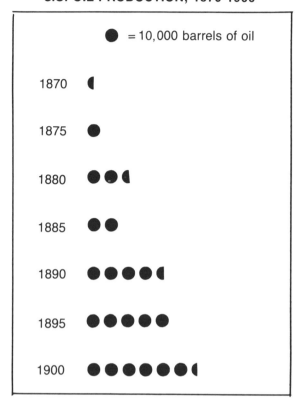

U.S. OIL PRODUCTION, 1870-1900

● = 10,000 barrels of oil

1870
1875
1880
1885
1890
1895
1900

1. Which years are shown in the charts?

_____

2. What does a square represent? _____

3. How many tons of steel were produced in 1870? _____

4. How many tons of steel were produced in 1880? _____

5. How many tons of steel were produced in 1900? _____

6. In which year was the most steel produced? _____

7. What does a circle represent? _____

8. How many barrels of oil were produced in 1880? _____

9. How many barrels of oil were produced in 1890? _____

10. How many more barrels of oil were produced in 1895 than in 1885?

_____

WRITING ACTIVITY.
Answer the questions with complete sentences.

1. What was an important invention of the 1800's?

_____

2. Who made this invention?

_____

3. How did this invention change people's lives?

_____

_____

4. Is this invention important today? Why or why not?

_____

_____

Describe an invention of the 1800's which is important to you. Use your answers to the above questions to write a paragraph. The title should be: An Important Invention For Me.

_____

_____

_____

_____

_____

_____

_____

_____

_____

_____

REVIEW EXERCISE.
Do you remember the meaning of the following words?
Thomas Edison, Alexander Graham Bell, Wilbur and Orville Wright, Andrew Carnegie, John D. Rockefeller

EARLY IMMIGRATION

PERSONAL SURVEY
Discuss these questions with your teacher and class.

1. What country did you or your family come from?
2. When did you or your family come to the U.S.?
3. Why did you or your family choose to come to the U.S.?
4. Do you or your family plan to return to your home country?
5. Where have you lived in the U.S.?

PRE-READING

Since the 1600's, people left their countries to move to the U.S. These people are called immigrants. Immigrants came to the U.S. for many reasons. Some came because of wars in their countries. Some came for religious freedom. Others came to find jobs and more opportunities. You will read about immigration in the U.S. in the 1800's in this lesson.

CONTENT VOCABULARY
These words are important in this lesson. What do you know about them?

Irish
German
Chinese
Ellis Island

SURVEY
Read the subtitles and the words in bold print. Look at the pictures.

1. What are some countries which the immigrants came from?
2. When did major immigrations occur?
3. Who passed immigration laws?

Look at the comprehension questions. Try to find the answers to these questions when you read the passage.

EARLY IMMIGRATION

Many Americans, except for the Native Americans, came from other countries. The first immigrants came from Europe. They came from England, the Netherlands, Spain, and France. Most Blacks came from Africa.

New Immigration Begins Between 1840 and 1870

More immigration began before the Civil War. In the 1840's and 1850's there was a pota famine in Ireland. Many people were starving because the potato was the main source of food. The **Irish** left their native country for the U.S. They were very poor. They saw the U.S as a chance for a new life. They moved to large cities and found unskilled jobs.

The **Germans** were the next major group to arrive at this time. The Germans were ofter skilled workers who started businesses. Some were farmers who started farms in the U.S. During the 1850's and the 1860's immigrants also came from China. Many came to work (the railroads. Others worked in the mines. The majority of the **Chinese** settled in the West especially in California.

adjustment (a change) During this first "wave" of new immigration more than five million people came. Each group experienced problems. There were cultural adjustments and many "Americans" did not like the "foreigners". However, the new country offered these groups many opportunities. These opportunities were better living conditions, jobs, and a chance to owr land.

Immigration Between 1870 and 1910

In 1870, the second "wave" of immigration occurred. People came to the U.S. for jobs. Most of the immigrants still came from Europe. They primarily came from England, the Netherlands, Sweden, and Norway.

In 1890, the immigration pattern changed. People started coming from other countries ir large numbers. They came from Italy, Bulgaria, Poland, Greece, and even Russia. Over sixteen million immigrants came during this second wave of immigration.

Ellis Island

The immigrants from Europe came to the U.S. by ship. They came through New York Ci Harbor. From 1892 to 1943, they stayed on an island that was called Ellis Island. Here, the presented the U.S. government with identification papers. They also received health tests. At one time, more than 5,000 people passed through Ellis Island in one day!

Congress Passes Immigration Laws

Many people in the U.S. became worried about the large numbers of immigrants who were coming into the U.S. Such people said the immigrants took their jobs, they brought poverty and crime, and they did not help the U.S. The government began to make laws to control immigration.

In 1917, Congress passed a law which said a person who could not read and write English could not enter the U.S. In 1924, the Congress passed the first **immigration quota.** *quota (a limit)* In 1929, the quota was 150,000 people each year. It also placed a percentage on the number of people who could come from different countries. At this time, 70% of the immigrants could come from Great Britain, Ireland, and Germany. There were no limits on immigration from Mexico, Central America or South America.

Summary

The immigrants who came to the U.S. wanted a better life. They brought different customs and languages. Congress passed laws which controlled the numbers of immigrants.

VOCABULARY EXERCISE

A. Read these verbs below. Find the correct nouns in the reading passage. Write them below.

VERB   NOUN

adjust   _____

immigrate   _____

farm   _____

work   _____

B. Read the sentences. Write the correct forms of the words.

1. Many _____ come to the U.S. every year.

2. Many immigrants have to _____ to the American culture.

3. Many immigrants came to _____

   or _____ in the United States.

COMPREHENSION EXERCISE.
Answer the questions.

1. What is the only non-immigrant group living in the U.S. today?

_____

_____

2. Why did the Irish immigrate to the U.S.?

_____

_____

3. Why do you think the Chinese immigrated to the U.S.?

_____

_____

4. Describe one immigration law passed after 1900.

_____

_____

5. What was one important change in the Immigration Law of 1924?

_____

_____

6. In 1924, were there any quotas on Mexican or South American immigrants?

_____

7. Why do you think some Americans were against some immigrants coming to the U.S.?

_____

_____

_____

8. How do you think the immigrants improved the U.S.?

_____

_____

_____

GRAMMAR EXERCISE.

CLAUSE CONNECTORS

The connectors **that, who,** and **which** can connect a clause to a sentence.
That and **who** connect a clause which is about people.
Example: The U.S. offered many opportunities to immigrants.
      The immigrants were poor.
      The U.S. offered many opportunities to immigrants who were poor.

That and **which** connect a clause which is about things.
Example: The immigrants came to Ellis Island.
      Ellis Island is in New York Harbor.
      The immigrants came to Ellis Island which is in New York Harbor.

A. Read the passage. Find sentences which contain the connectors ''that'', ''who'', and ''which''. Copy them below.

1. that _____

_____

2. who _____

_____

3. which _____

_____

B. Read the sentences. Combine them with "who" or "which".

1. The U.S. offered opportunities to many people.

   These people were often poor.

   _____

   _____

2. There were two waves of immigration.

   The waves brought many people to the U.S.

   _____

   _____

3. The first wave occurred between 1840 and 1870.

   It brought five million immigrants.

   _____

   _____

4. Many German immigrants came to the U.S.

   They were skilled workers and farmers.

   _____

   _____

5. Most European immigrants came to Ellis Island.

   It is located in New York Harbor.

   _____

   _____

C. Write two sentences. One sentence should have "who" and the other "which". Use the information from this lesson.

1. _____

   _____

2. _____

   _____

GRAPHICAL LITERACY.
Look at the charts. Answer the questions.

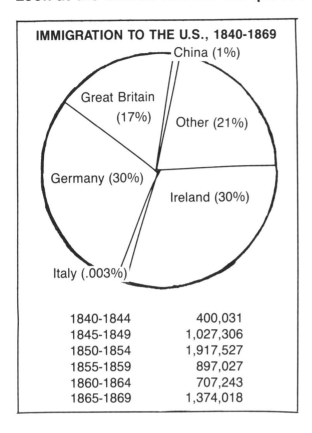

IMMIGRATION TO THE U.S., 1840-1869

China (1%)
Great Britain (17%)
Other (21%)
Germany (30%)
Ireland (30%)
Italy (.003%)

1840-1844	400,031
1845-1849	1,027,306
1850-1854	1,917,527
1855-1859	897,027
1860-1864	707,243
1865-1869	1,374,018

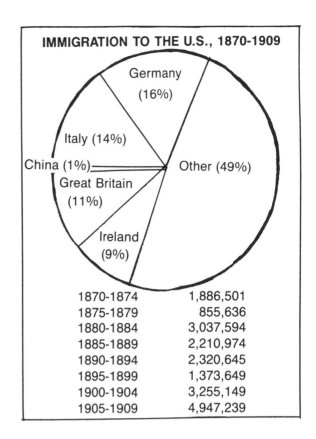

IMMIGRATION TO THE U.S., 1870-1909

Germany (16%)
Italy (14%)
China (1%)
Great Britain (11%)
Other (49%)
Ireland (9%)

1870-1874	1,886,501
1875-1879	855,636
1880-1884	3,037,594
1885-1889	2,210,974
1890-1894	2,320,645
1895-1899	1,373,649
1900-1904	3,255,149
1905-1909	4,947,239

1. How many people came to the U.S. from 1840 to 1844? _____

2. How many people came to the U.S. from 1860 to 1864? _____

3. How many immigrants came from 1855 to 1859? _____

4. How many immigrants came from 1840 to 1869? _____

5. What percent of all immigrants from 1840 to 1869 came from Germany? _____

6. What percent of all immigrants from 1840 to 1869 came from Ireland

   and Great Britain? _____

7. How many immigrants came from 1890 to 1894? _____

8. How many immigrants came from 1900 to 1904? _____

9. How many immigrants came from 1900 to 1909? _____

10. What is the total number of immigrants who came from 1870 to 1909? _____

11. From 1840 to 1869, where did the largest percent of immigrants come from? _____

12. What percent of immigrants came from **Ireland** from 1840 to 1869? _____

13. What percent of immigrants came from Ireland from 1870 to 1909? _____

WRITING ACTIVITY.
Answer the questions with complete sentences.

1. What was an important immigrant group in the 1800's?

_____

2. Why did this group come to the U.S.?

_____

_____

3. Was life better for them in the U.S. than in their native country? Why or why not?

_____

_____

Describe one important immigrant group. Use your answers to the above questions to write a paragraph. The title should be: An Immigrant Group of the 1800's.

_____

_____

_____

_____

_____

_____

_____

_____

_____

_____

_____

_____

REVIEW EXERCISE.
Do you remember the meaning of the following words?
Irish, German, Chinese, Ellis Island, immigration quota

WORLD WAR I

PERSONAL SURVEY
Discuss these questions with your teacher and class.

1. What do you think about when you read the words "World War"?
2. What does "neutral" mean?
3. If your best friend were in a fight, would you help your friend? Why or why not?

PRE-READING

Many countries fought in World War I. At first, the U.S. did not want to enter the war. It wanted to stay neutral. Finally, the U.S. had to enter the war. The U.S. fought with the Allies against Germany and the other Central Powers. You will read about the war in this lesson.

CONTENT VOCABULARY
These words are important in this lesson. What do you know about them?

Allies
Central Powers
Woodrow Wilson
League of Nations

SURVEY
Read the first paragraph, the subtitles, the words in bold print, and the summary. Look at the pictures.

1. When did the war start?
2. How did the war start?
3. On which side did the U.S. fight?

Look at the comprehension questions. Try to find the answers to these questions when you read the passage.

WORLD WAR I

In 1914, **Archduke Ferdinand,** a prince from Austria-Hungary, and his wife were assassinated. Austria blamed its neighbor, Serbia, for the murders. Soon, other European countries became involved. There were two sides. One side was called the **Central Powers** which included Germany, Austria-Hungary, Turkey, and Bulgaria. The other side was called the **Allies** which included Great Britain, Russia, Japan, France, and Italy and later the U.S.

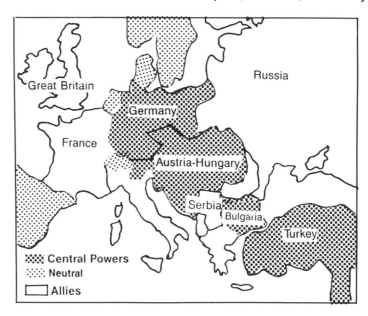

The U.S. Tries To Remain Neutral

President Woodrow Wilson was re-elected in 1916 because he promised the American people to "keep us out of war". However, it became very difficult to remain neutral. The U.S. sent food and manufactured products to the Allies. They sent these goods by ship to Europe. The Central Powers wanted to stop the delivery of these goods. The Central Powers *submarine* had **submarines.** These submarines sank many U.S. ships which were carrying goods to *(an* the Allies. Many Americans died on these ships. Finally, in 1917, the U.S. declared war on *underwater* the Central Powers. The U.S. felt that the Central Powers were against democracy. The goal *ship)* of the U.S. was to "make the world safe for democracy".

The U.S. Prepares for War

The U.S. government needed money, soldiers, and war materials. The government sold Liberty Bonds to help pay for the war. U.S. factories built ships, submarines, and weapons to fight the war. Congress passed the **Selective Service Act** on May 18, 1917. This act was *register* also known as the **draft.** Under this law, men had to register for military service. By June *(to enroll)* 1917, more than 9,500,000 had registered for military service!

The U.S. Stops German Submarines

German submarines sank many Allied ships. The U.S. began to produce small ships called subchasers. These ships had underwater listening devices. These devices helped the subchasers find the submarines when they were under the sea. The subchasers also had depth charges. They dropped these explosives into the sea. They fell to the bottom of the sea and exploded. The subchasers followed the German submarines and destroyed them. Soon, the U.S. was sinking the submarines faster than Germany could build them!

Americans firing at German Airplanes

The U.S. Joins the Allies in Europe

In early 1918, the Allies were in trouble. Russia's new Communist government surrendered to Germany. The German Army left Russia and returned to Europe to fight the British and French. The Americans soon began to help the French and the British.

By July of 1918, the Allies' situation improved. First, the Allies defeated Germany at Cantigny, France. At the same time, France kept Germany from reaching Paris. The Allies defeated Germany at the famous Argonne Forest Battle. Finally, on November 11, 1918, World War I ended. There was an armistice. The final peace treaty, the **Treaty of Versailles,** was signed in June, 1919.

The U.S. And World Peace

World problems continued after World War I. Germany and the other Central Powers had many war debts. They owed a lot of money to the Allies. The economies in these countries were very bad. Germany and the others stopped paying their debts.

President Wilson was worried about world peace. He helped create the **League of** *create (to make)* **Nations.** Many countries were members of this organization. They met to talk about peace and to solve problems in the world.

Summary

World War I began in Europe. In the beginning, the U.S. tried to remain neutral. Soon the U.S. joined the war with the Allies. The Allies won the war. Even though the Allies won the war, there were still many problems in the world.

VOCABULARY EXERCISE
Read the words. Write the correct words in the sentences.

submarine	register	create	draft
democracy	armistice	neutral	war debts

1. A _____ country chooses not to fight on any side in a war.

2. An _____ is an agreement for peace.

3. People elect their government representatives in a _____.

4. A _____ can travel under the water.

5. Men had to _____ for military service.

6. After World War I, countries had to pay their _____.

7. Congress created the _____ in 1917 in order to get more soldiers.

8. President Wilson helped to _____ the League of Nations.

COMPREHENSION EXERCISE.
Answer the questions.

1. Which countries were a part of the Central Powers?

_____

_____

2. Which countries were a part of the Allies?

_____

_____

3. Why did the U.S. enter World War I?

_____

_____

4. How did the U.S. prepare for World War I?

_____

_____

_____

_____

5. What was the draft?

_____

_____

6. Who won World War I?

_____

_____

7. Did World War I solve the problems in the world? Why or why not?

_____

_____

8. Should a country that wins a war force the losing country to pay a war debt? Why or why not?

_____

_____

9. What do you think a world peace organization should do?

_____

_____

GRAMMAR EXERCISE.

PRONOUNS		
Subject	Possessive	Object
He	his	him
She	her	her
It	its	it
They	their	them

A. Read the passage. Find sentences with "he", "they", and "them". Copy them below.

1. he _____

_____

2. they _____

_____

3. them _____

_____

B. Rewrite the sentences below using words which the pronouns refer to.

1. <u>He</u> was assassinated in 1914.

_____

2. <u>She</u> was assassinated in 1914.

_____

3. <u>It</u> began when Austria-Hungary fought against Serbia.

_____

4. <u>It</u> wanted to stay neutral.

_____

5. The U.S. sent <u>them</u> by ship to Europe.

_____

6. <u>They</u> sank many U.S. ships which had products for Europe.

_____

7. <u>They</u> followed the German submarines and destroyed <u>them.</u>

_____

8. <u>They</u> fought very hard on the Western Front.

_____

9. <u>It</u> ended on November 11, 1918.

_____

10. <u>He</u> helped create the League of Nations.

_____

C. Write two sentences. Use the pronouns ''they'' and ''them''. Use the information in this lesson.

1. they _____

_____

2. them _____

_____

GRAPHICAL LITERACY.
Read the timelines. Answer the questions.

WORLD WAR I TIMELINES

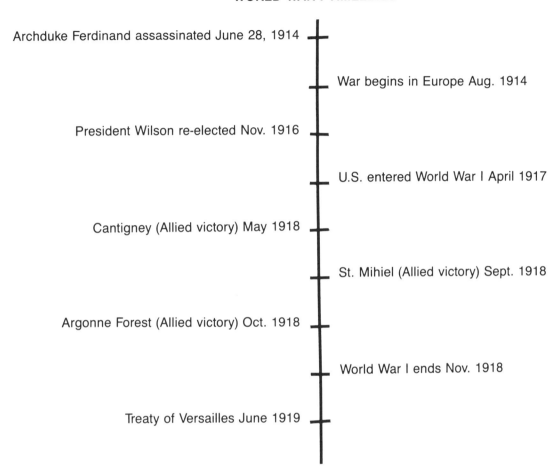

Archduke Ferdinand assassinated June 28, 1914

War begins in Europe Aug. 1914

President Wilson re-elected Nov. 1916

U.S. entered World War I April 1917

Cantigney (Allied victory) May 1918

St. Mihiel (Allied victory) Sept. 1918

Argonne Forest (Allied victory) Oct. 1918

World War I ends Nov. 1918

Treaty of Versailles June 1919

1. When does the timeline begin? _____

2. When does the timeline end? _____

3. What is the first event? _____

4. When was President Wilson re-elected? _____

5. When did the U.S. enter World War I? _____

6. Name two major Allied victories. _____

_____

7. When did World War I end? _____

8. How long did the U.S. fight in the war? _____

9. When was the Treaty of Versailles signed? _____

WRITING ACTIVITY.
Answer the questions with complete sentences.

1. How did the U.S. prepare for war? List at least three activities.

_____

_____

_____

2. Why was each activity important?

_____

_____

_____

Describe how the U.S. prepared for World War I. Use your answers to the above questions to write a paragraph. The title should be: The U.S. Prepared for World War I.

_____

_____

_____

_____

_____

_____

_____

_____

_____

_____

_____

_____

REVIEW EXERCISE.
Do you remember the meaning of the following words?
Central Powers, Allies, Woodrow Wilson, Selective Service Act, Treaty of Versailles, League of Nations

GOOD TIMES AND BAD TIMES

PERSONAL SURVEY
Discuss these questions with your teacher and class.

1. Do you know anyone who does not have a job?
2. What problems does an unemployed person have?
3. How does an unemployed person get food? Clothing? A home? Money?

PRE-READING

After World War I, unemployment increased in the U.S. During the 1920's, the U.S. economy improved. People had jobs and they could buy many things. In the 1930's, the economy became bad. Many people lost their jobs. The Great Depression arrived. You will read about the "good times" and the "bad times" in this lesson.

CONTENT VOCABULARY
These words are important in this lesson. What do you know about them?

Eighteenth Amendment
Susan B. Anthony
Roaring Twenties
Crash of 1929
the Great Depression

SURVEY
Read the first paragraph, the subtitles, the words in bold print, and the summary. Look at the pictures.

1. When were the good times in the U.S.?
2. When were the bad times in the U.S.?

Look at the comprehension questions. Try to find the answers to these questions when you read the passage.

GOOD TIMES AND BAD TIMES

The U.S. had good times and bad times after World War I. First, there was the Postwar Depression, then came the Roaring Twenties, and then the Great Depression.

The Postwar Depression

There were some economic problems after World War I. The U.S. shifted from a wartime economy to a peacetime economy. The U.S. government cancelled many wartime contracts with companies that produced ships, airplanes, and war materials. Many workers were laid off. Sometimes workers' salaries were reduced. Many veterans could not find work when they returned to the U.S. after the war.

The Roaring Twenties

Before 1920, women were not allowed to vote in the U.S. As early as the 1860's, women such as **Susan B. Anthony** tried to get women the right to vote. Women played a very important role in helping the U.S. win World War I. They worked in many factories that made war materials. Because of their work, many people were convinced that women should have

equal (the same) equal voting rights. In 1920, the **Nineteenth Amendment** was passed. It guaranteed women the right to vote in all states.

People demonstrating for voting rights for women

In the 1920's, the U.S. economy began to improve. Workers began to find jobs. People began to spend money again. Henry Ford was producing many automobiles. Workers were

assemble (to put together) assembling the automobiles on assembly lines. The cars were inexpensive and people could afford them. Radio and movie theaters also became popular. Many inventions, such as the electric washing machine, the refrigerator, and the vaccuum cleaner made life easier. Stores started to offer installment or time payment plans. **Consumers** bought many products because of the availability of the installment plans.

At this time, people bought many **stocks.** A stock is a part of a company. A person could own a part of a company by buying some company stocks. When the company made money, the price of the stocks would increase. The people who owned the stocks and who sold them made money. If the value of the stocks decreased, the stock owners would lose money if they sold them. In the early 1920's, many people who bought and sold stocks made a profit because the companies made money. In the late 1920's, many people borrowed money to buy many stocks. They thought they could make a lot of money.

A failed bank, 1936

Dust storm in Oklahoma, 1936

The Great Depression

On October 29, 1929 the **Crash of 1929** came. The prices of stocks decreased very fast. Many people who owned stocks lost millions of dollars because their stocks had lost their value. The **Great Depression** began.

Many other terrible things happened to the economy. People went to the banks to withdraw their money. The banks ran out of money and failed. They failed because they had invested their customers' money in stocks. They lost their customers' money.

Many people were unemployed. They had no money. They lost their savings when the *unemployed* banks failed. They could not pay their debts. Farmers were in trouble because they had *(not working)* borrowed a lot of money to pay for seed, fertilizer, and new equipment. Because of the dry weather and poor farming methods, there were large "dust bowls". Strong winds blew the good soil away. Farmers did not have good crops. Many farmers lost their farms. Many people blamed **President Herbert Hoover** for all these problems.

Summary

After World War I, there was a postwar depression. Then came the Roaring Twenties. People had jobs. Consumers spent money on many products. Many people bought stocks and made a lot of money. The Great Depression started in 1929 when the stock market crashed. Banks, farms, and companies failed. People lost their jobs. In 1932, Americans elected Franklin Delano Roosevelt President. They hoped he would end the Great Depression and bring more good times to the U.S.

VOCABULARY EXERCISE
Read the words. Write the words next to the definitions.

a contract   equal   a consumer   unemployed
a veteran   to assemble   a stock

1. _____ The same.

2. _____ A person who fought in a war.

3. _____ Without a job.

4. _____ To put together.

5. _____ A legal agreement to make a product or give a service.

6. _____ A document that shows a part ownership in a company.

7. _____ A person who buys things.

COMPREHENSION EXERCISE.
Answer the questions.

1. What do factories produce in a "wartime economy"?

_____

_____

2. What rights did the Nineteenth Amendment guarantee?

_____

_____

3. How did Henry Ford make automobiles quickly?

_____

_____

4. What is a consumer?

_____

_____

5. What is a stock?

_____

_____

6. How did people make money with stocks?

_____

_____

7. What happened to the stock market during the Great Depression?

_____

_____

8. What happened to the banks during the Great Depression?

_____

_____

9. How did the bank failures affect people in the U.S.?

_____

_____

10. Why do you think people blamed President Herbert Hoover for the problems in the U.S.?

_____

_____

_____

GRAMMAR EXERCISE.

BECAUSE and BECAUSE OF

Because and **because of** are used to show reasons.

Because of is used with a noun phrase.
Example: Women could vote because of the Nineteenth Amendment.

NOTE: If the phrase is at the beginning of the sentence, use a comma after it.
Example: Because of the Nineteenth Amendment, women could vote.

Because is used with a clause.
Example: Women could vote because Congress passed the Nineteenth Amendment.

NOTE: If the clause is at the beginning of the sentence, use a comma after it.
Example: Because Congress passed the Nineteenth Amendment, women could vote.

A. Read the passage. Find sentences with ''because'' and ''because of''. Copy them below.

1. because _____

_____

2. because of _____

_____

B. Complete the sentences. Use ''because'' or ''because of''.

1. The U.S. had economic problems after World War I _____

the economy shifted to peacetime work.

2. Many workers were laid off _____ companies stopped producing war

materials.

3. Women could vote _____ the Nineteenth Amendment.

4. _____ the economy improved, people got jobs.

C. Complete the sentences. Use the information from this lesson.

1. Banks failed because _____

_____

2. Farmers lost their farms because _____

_____

3. Farmers could not grow crops because of _____

_____

4. Many people could not pay their debts because _____

_____

D. Write two sentences. Write one sentence with ''because'' and the other with ''because of''. Use the information from this lesson.

1. because _____

_____

2. because of _____

_____

GRAPHICAL LITERACY.
Look at the chart. Answer the questions.

UNEMPLOYMENT, 1920-1935

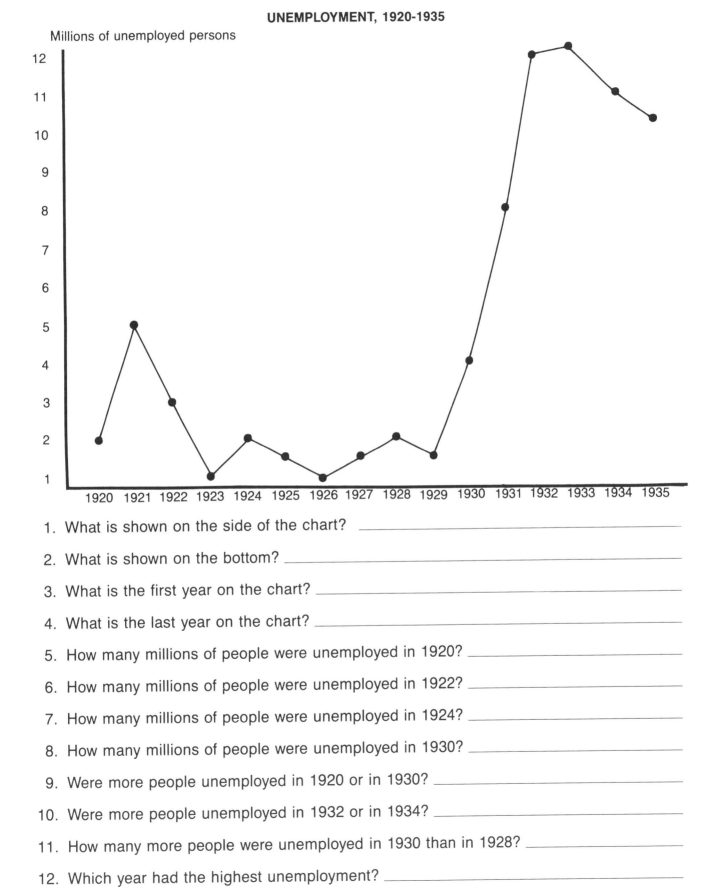

Millions of unemployed persons

1. What is shown on the side of the chart? _____

2. What is shown on the bottom? _____

3. What is the first year on the chart? _____

4. What is the last year on the chart? _____

5. How many millions of people were unemployed in 1920? _____

6. How many millions of people were unemployed in 1922? _____

7. How many millions of people were unemployed in 1924? _____

8. How many millions of people were unemployed in 1930? _____

9. Were more people unemployed in 1920 or in 1930? _____

10. Were more people unemployed in 1932 or in 1934? _____

11. How many more people were unemployed in 1930 than in 1928? _____

12. Which year had the highest unemployment? _____

WRITING ACTIVITY.
Answer the questions with complete sentences.

1. What were three causes of the Great Depression?

_____

_____

_____

2. What happened because of each reason listed above?

_____

_____

_____

You are writing a newspaper article. You want to describe the causes of the Great Depression. The title of your article is: Why The Great Depression Happened.

_____

New York   July 28, 1931

by _____

_____

_____

_____

_____

_____

_____

_____

_____

_____

REVIEW EXERCISE.
Do you remember the meaning of the following words?
Susan B. Anthony, Nineteenth Amendment, stocks, Crash of 1929, the Great Depression

UNIT REVIEW
Describe the importance of each person, document, or event.

1. Thomas Alva Edison

_____

_____

2. immigration quota

_____

_____

3. World War I

_____

_____

4. Treaty of Versailles

_____

_____

5. Nineteenth Amendment

_____

_____

6. Crash of 1929

_____

_____

7. the Great Depression

_____

_____

IMPORTANT TIMES
Write the important event that happened in each of these years.

Dec. 17, 1903 _____

1914-1919 _____

1920 _____

1924 _____

Oct. 29, 1929 _____

1932 _____

UNIT FOUR

THE NEW DEAL

WORLD WAR II

THE UNITED NATIONS

THE NEW DEAL

PERSONAL SURVEY
Discuss these questions with your teacher and class.

1. Do you know anyone who gets social security?
2. Do you know anyone who gets assistance from the government?
   What do they receive?
3. Do you know anyone who works in a government program?
   What do they do?

PRE-READING

In the 1930's, many Americans needed help. The economy was weak. More than 14 million people were unemployed. Thousands of people lost their homes. President Roosevelt tried to help Americans. He created the New Deal. You will read about the New Deal in this lesson.

CONTENT VOCABULARY
These words are important in this lesson. What do you know about them?

New Deal
Bank Holiday
Social Security Act

SURVEY
Read the first paragraph, the subtitles, the words in bold print, and the summary. Look at the pictures.

1. Who did the New Deal help?

Look at the comprehension questions. Try to find the answers to these questions when you read the passage.

THE NEW DEAL

Franklin Delano Roosevelt (FDR) had a plan to end the problems of the Great Depression. His plan which was called the **New Deal** provided help to people without food, housing, or jobs. It also provided help to businesses. It also created new laws which tried to prevent another depression.

Franklin Delano Roosevelt, talking to voters, 1936

Banks Receive Assistance

FDR made a bank holiday. He closed all the banks in the U.S. Inspectors came to each bank and checked the bank's records. Banks which were in good financial condition were re-opened. FDR wanted people to have confidence in the banks. He created a new federal agency which was called the **Federal Deposit Insurance Corporation** (FDIC). This agency insured all bank deposits. It guaranteed people their money if a bank closed.

The Unemployed Receive Assistance

Congress gave more than three billion dollars to the **Public Works Administration** (PWA). The PWA hired hundreds of unemployed people to build bridges, dams, buildings, and highways.

Congress created the **Civilian Conservation Corps** (CCC) to help unemployed young people. The people who the CCC hired worked in national parks. They planted trees, fought forest fires, and worked on irrigation projects.

Unemployed and Retired Workers Receive Assistance

The **Social Security Act** was another important law which helped unemployed and older workers. Under this law, employers and workers paid social security insurance. This plan paid benefits to a person who lost a job or retired after the age of 65.

Farmers Receive Assistance

There was a surplus of many farm products. Farmers could not sell many products. The products which they sold had low prices. Some farmers were becoming very poor. The **Agricultural Adjustment Act** (AAA) helped farmers. Under this law, the government bought surplus food which it gave to the poor. The government also paid farmers not to plant certain crops.

surplus (extra)

Paying For the New Deal

The New Deal was expensive. The government borrowed money to pay for the New Deal. It also established an **income tax** which businesses and individuals had to pay. It taxed businesses' profits and individuals' income.

income (the money a person earns)

Summary

The New Deal helped to solve the problems of the Great Depression. With new laws, the Federal government helped many people. Many of these New Deal programs are still available today.

AN IMPORTANT PERSON IN U.S. HISTORY: Eleanor Roosevelt

Eleanor Roosevelt was born in New York City in 1884. She did not have a happy childhood. When Eleanor was eight years old, her mother and brother died. Soon after, her father died. When Eleanor was fifteen years old, she went to school in England. Her uncle, Theodore Roosevelt, was President when she returned.

Eleanor married Franklin Delano Roosevelt. They had five children. Franklin was active in politics. In fact, he ran for Vice-President in 1920, but he lost the election. One day, after swimming, Franklin became sick. He had polio! Because of the disease, he lost the use of his legs. Eleanor encouraged her husband to continue in politics. She helped him to win the election for Governor of New York in 1929. Finally, in 1932, he was elected President. Eleanor became the First Lady.

Eleanor was a busy First Lady. She travelled around the U.S. She talked to farmers, coal miners, and people from all parts of the U.S. She began to work with Black leaders to obtain equal rights for Blacks. During World War II, she travelled all over the world to visit American soldiers. Because of her work, she was very popular with the people in the U.S.

After Eleanor's husband died, she continued her work. She continued to work for human rights for the poor and disadvantaged in the U.S. and in the entire world. She died in 1962.

VOCABULARY EXERCISE
Read these words. Write the correct words in the sentences. Use each word only one time.

incomes   unemployed   benefits   surplus   assistance   profits

1. The New Deal provided _____ to many Americans who needed help.

2. The government bought _____ crops from farmers and gave the food to the poor.

3. The Federal Government began to tax business _____ and

   individuals' _____.

4. The Social Security Act pays a person _____ after the person retires.

5. The Public Works Administration and the Civilian Conservation Corps hired

   _____ people.

COMPREHENSION EXERCISE.
Answer the questions.

1. Who created the New Deal?

   _____

2. What did the Federal Insurance Deposit Corporation do?

   _____

   _____

3. Which two programs created jobs?

   _____

   _____

4. What did the Social Security Act do?

   _____

   _____

5. What did the Agricultural Adjustment Act do?

   _____

   _____

6. Where did the money for the New Deal come from?

_____

_____

7. Do you think everyone liked the New Deal programs? Why or why not?

_____

_____

8. Which programs today are similar to the New Deal programs?

_____

_____

GRAMMAR EXERCISE.

CONNECTORS

The connectors **who** and **which** can connect sentences.

Who refers to people.
Example: The farmers respected Eleanor Roosevelt.
        Eleanor helped them.
        The farmers who Eleanor helped respected her.

NOTE: Sometimes "whom" is used if the connector is an object. Today, "who" is used usually for both subject and object positions.

Which refers to things.
Example: The New Deal helped the end the Depression.
        FDR planned the New Deal.
        The New Deal, which FDR planned, helped to end the Depression.

A. Read the passage. Find a sentence with "who" and another sentence with "which". Copy them below.

1. who _____

_____

2. which _____

_____

B. Combine the sentences. Use "who" or "which".

1. The New Deal was important.

   FDR created the New Deal.

   _____

   _____

2. The New Deal consisted of many projects.

   FDR created the projects to help people.

   _____

   _____

3. An important law was the Social Security Act.

   Congress passed the Social Security Act in 1935.

   _____

   _____

4. The government established the income tax.

   Individuals and businesses had to pay the income tax.

   _____

   _____

5. Eleanor Roosevelt died in 1962.

   People liked her very much.

   _____

   _____

C. Write a sentence. Use either "who" or "which". Use the information from this lesson.

   _____

   _____

   _____

   _____

GRAPHICAL LITERACY.
Look at the table. Answer the questions.

NEW DEAL LEGISLATION		
Laws	**Year**	**Description**
Federal Deposit Insurance Corporation	1933	Guaranteed depositors money if banks closed
Public Works Administration	1933	Employed people to build bridges, roads, and dams
Civilian Conservation Corps	1933	Employed young people in National Parks to plant trees, fight forest fires, and work on irrigation projects
Agriculture Adjustment Act	1933	Bought surplus crops from farmers
Social Security Act	1935	Provided benefits to the unemployed and retired
Works Progress Administration	1935	Created jobs for building schools

1. How many laws are listed in the table? _____

2. Which years are listed in the table? _____

3. In which year was most of the New Deal legislation passed? _____

4. Which two laws were passed in 1935? _____

_____

5. Which New Deal programs provided jobs? _____

_____

_____

6. Which New Deal law helped the retired? _____

_____

7. Which New Deal law helped the banks? _____

_____

8. How did the Agriculture Adjustment Act help farmers? _____

_____

_____

_____

_____

WRITING ACTIVITY.

Pretend you are one of the following:

Mary Miller, a farmer's wife

Jim Smith, an 18 year old unemployed high school graduate

Bill Anderson, a 30 year old unemployed factory worker

Laura Jones, a 66 year old retired office worker.

Choose one of the New Deal programs which helped you. Write a paragraph about this program. Explain how it helped your life. The title of your paragraph should be: How the New Deal Helped Me.

Signature _____

REVIEW EXERCISE.

Do you remember the meaning of the following words?

Franklin Delano Roosevelt, Eleanor Roosevelt, New Deal, Social Security Act, income tax

WORLD WAR II

PERSONAL SURVEY
Discuss these questions with your teacher and class.

1. What do you think happened during World War II?
2. Do you know anyone who fought in World War II?
   Where did they fight?
3. Do you know the names of any world leaders from World War II?
   Which countries were they from?

PRE-READING
There were many problems in the world during the 1930's. Some countries had leaders who wanted to control the land and people of neighboring countries. Because of this, World War II began. You will read about World War II in this lesson.

CONTENT VOCABULARY
These words are important in this lesson. What do you know about them?

Mussolini
Hitler
Nazi Party
Axis Powers
Allied Powers
Pearl Harbor
Douglas MacArthur
Dwight D. Eisenhower

SURVEY
Read the first paragraph, the subtitles, the words in bold print, and the summary. Look at the pictures.

1. What were the two sides in World War II called?
2. Where was World War II fought?
3. When did the war end?

Look at the comprehension questions. Try to find the answers to these questions when you read the passage.

WORLD WAR II

In the 1930's, serious problems appeared in the world. Totalitarian governments were se up in Japan, Germany, and Italy. In these countries, the government controlled the people lives. People did not have many rights. Government power was held by one person or a small group of people. A government operated by one person is called a dictatorship. In tl 1930's, totalitarian governments threatened small neighboring countries. Another world wa was beginning.

The Axis Powers

Just before World War II, there were several very strong totalitarian governments. In Ital **Benito Mussolini** began with his **Fascist Party.** Shortly after, **Adolf Hitler** and his **Nazi Party** came to power in Germany. The Nazi Party killed and tortured millions of people. In fact, the Nazis tried to destroy the Jewish people. A third totalitarian government was in Japan. In the 1930's, these three countries—Italy, Germany, and Japan, joined forces. The became known as the Axis Powers.

The Neutrality Act

arms (weapons, guns, etc.)

In 1935, the U.S. Congress passed the **Neutrality Act.** This law said the U.S. could not sell arms to other nations at war. As World War II neared, it became difficult for the U.S. government to obey this law.

World War II Begins in Asia

In 1937, Japan invaded China. The U.S. was neutral. It did not want to send arms to China. There was a great debate. After the debate, the U.S. government finally agreed to sell arms to other countries. The other countries had to pay cash for these arms. Some countries had difficulty buying the arms because they did not have the money.

World War II Begins in Europe

After Germany attacked Poland in 1939, France and England declared war on Germany France and England were called the **Allied Powers.** Russia supported Germany and the Axis Powers until Germany attacked Russia. After Germany's attack, Russia changed side and joined the Allies.

The U.S. Joins the War

During this time, the U.S. government was trying to remain neutral. The U.S. did not wa to get involved in the war until Japan attacked a U.S. naval base at **Pearl Harbor,** Hawaii December 7, 1941. After Pearl Harbor, the U.S. declared war on Japan and the other Axis Powers.

The Pacific Front

World War II was fought on two fronts. It was fought in Europe and in the Pacific. Japan was very powerful in the Pacific. Before the U.S. entered the war, Japan had conquered many islands in the Pacific Ocean. The U.S. Army was led by General Douglas MacArthu Admiral Chester W. Nimitz led the U.S. Navy. These men won many battles in the Pacific i early 1944 and 1945. While the Navy was fighting in the Pacific, the U.S. Air Force was bombing large industrial cities in Japan.

A damaged American ship.

The Western Front

During the early days of World War II, Germany and the other Axis Powers were winning easily. Germany bombed both England and France. It appeared as though the Axis Powers would win the war.

Finally, the Allies defeated the Germans in North Africa. The Allies were led by General **Dwight D. Eisenhower.** In 1943, the Allies defeated the Axis Powers in Italy. After this, the Allies won many battles in France. They forced the Germans to retreat to Germany. The Russians won battles against Germany in Eastern Europe.

retreat (to go back)

World War II Ends

Finally, on May 7, 1945, World War II ended in Europe. Germany, the last Axis Power, surrendered to the Allies. However, the war on the Pacific Front still continued. In 1945, Japan was losing many battles to the Allies. The Allies were also bombing Japanese cities. In August 1945, the U.S. had a secret plan to end the war with Japan. They planed to drop two **atomic bombs** on Japan. The atomic bombs were new. On August 6, and August 9, 1945, the bombs were dropped on two industrial cities of Japan, **Hiroshima** and **Nagasaki.** These bombs killed thousands of people instantly!

After the great destruction from these bombs, the war against Japan ended quickly. On September 2, 1945, Japan surrendered and World War II ended. Now, the world had to rebuild from the terrible effects of another world war.

Summary

Before World War II, the U.S. tried to remain neutral. As in World War I, the U.S. soon joined its allies. Many people from many countries died in World War II. The Allies won the war after two atomic bombs were dropped in Japan.

VOCABULARY EXERCISE
Read these words. Write the words next to their definitions.

a dictator   arms   to invade   to retreat   an atomic bomb

1. _____ A person who operates the government. This person is not elected by the people.

2. _____ To go back.

3. _____ Guns and other weapons.

4. _____ A very powerful weapon. It helped to end World War II.

5. _____ To enter another country with an army.

COMPREHENSION EXERCISE.
Answer the questions.

1. What is a totalitarian government?

_____

_____

2. Who were three major Axis countries?

_____

_____

3. Who were three major Allies?

_____

_____

4. On which side did Russia first fight?

_____

_____

5. Why did Russia join the Allies?

_____

_____

6. When did the Allies begin to win the war?

_____

_____

7. Did the atomic bomb end the war in Europe?

_____

8. Do you think the atomic bomb was necessary to end World War II? Why or why not?

_____

_____

GRAMMAR EXERCISE.

CONNECTORS

Connecting words often show time relationships.
Before is used with phrases and clauses.
Example: Before Pearl Harbor, the U.S. was neutral.
Before Japan attacked Pearl Harbor, the U.S. was neutral.

After is used with phrases and clauses.
Example: After Pearl Harbor, the U.S. declared war on Japan.
After Japan attacked Pearl Harbor, the U.S. declared war.

Until is used with phrases and clauses.
Example: Russia supported Germany until the German invasion.
Russia supported Germany until Germany invaded.

During is used with a phrase and while is used with a clause.
Example: Many people died during World War II.
Many people died while the armies were fighting in World War II.

A. Read the passage. Find sentences with "before," "after", "during", and "while". Copy them.

1. before _____

_____

2. after _____

_____

3. during _____

_____

4. while _____

_____

B. Write the correct connectors.

England declared war _____ Germany attacked Poland. Russia joined the

Allies _____ Germany attacked Russia. The U.S. was neutral

_____ Pearl Harbor. People from many countries died _____ this

war.

C. Complete the sentences.

1. Japan won many battles in the Pacific before _____

_____

2. The U.S. was neutral until _____

_____

3. The U.S. declared war on Japan after _____

_____

4. General MacArthur and Admiral Nimitz won many battles during _____

_____

5. The U.S. was bombing Japanese cities while _____

_____

6. The Japanese surrendered after _____

_____

D. Write two sentences. Use ''before'' and ''after''. Use the information in this lesson.

1. before _____

_____

_____

2. after _____

_____

_____

GRAPHICAL LITERACY.
Read the timelines. Answer the questions.

WORLD WAR II TIMELINES

1937
Japan invades China

June 1940
France surrenders to Germany

Sept. 1943
Italy surrenders to Allies

May 1945
Allies defeat Germany

Sept. 1945
Japan surrenders

1939
War begins in Europe

Dec. 7, 1941
Pearl Harbor;
U.S. enters World War II

Aug.-Sept., 1944
Allies free France,
Belgium, and Luxemburg

Aug. 1945
U.S. drops atomic bombs

1. When did Japan invade China? _____

_____

2. When did World War II begin in Europe? _____

_____

3. When did the Allies begin to win the war? _____

_____

4. When did the U.S. drop the atomic bombs on Japan? _____

_____

5. When did Japan surrender to the Allies? _____

_____

6. Did Italy surrender before Germany? _____

7. Did Japan surrender after Germany? _____

8. Did Italy surrender before Japan? _____

WRITING ACTIVITY.
Answer the questions with complete sentences.

1. Identify an event which helped the Allies win the war. Describe why it was important.

_____

_____

2. Identify a second event which helped the Allies win the war. Describe why it was important.

_____

_____

3. Identify a third event which helped the allies to win the war. Describe why it was important.

_____

_____

Pretend you are a general in the U.S. Army at the end of the war. Write a letter to President Truman. Describe why the Allies won the war. Use your answers.

President Harry S. Truman   **Nov. 13, 1945**
White House
Washington D.C.

Dear Mr. President:

_____

_____

_____

_____

_____

_____

_____

                                    Sincerely,

                        _____

REVIEW EXERCISE.
Do you remember the meaning of following words?
Axis Powers, Allied Powers, Benito Mussolini, Adolf Hitler, Nazi Party, Pearl Harbor, Dwight D. Eisenhower, Hiroshima and Nagasaki

THE UNITED NATIONS

PERSONAL SURVEY
Discuss these questions with your teacher and class.

1. What does a world peace organization do?

PRE-READING

After World War II, many countries wanted world peace. They set up a world organization called the United Nations. Its goal was to maintain world peace. You will read about the United Nations in this lesson.

CONTENT VOCABULARY
These words are important in this lesson. What do you know about them?

United Nations
Korean War

SURVEY
Read the first paragraph, the subtitles, the words in bold print, and the summary. Look at the pictures.

1. What are the names of some departments of the United Nations?
2. In which war was the United Nations involved?

Look at the comprehension questions. Try to find the answers to these questions when you read the passage.

THE UNITED NATIONS

During the war, many leaders thought about world peace. From August 24 to October 7, 1944 representatives from China, Great Britain, Russia, and the U.S. met and discussed a world peace organization. Later in February 1945, Winston Churchill from Great Britain, Joseph Stalin from Russia, and President Roosevelt made plans for the United Nations.

The United Nations

The United Nations Is Established

In April, 1945 representatives from more than fifty countries met in San Francisco, California. The final plans for the United Nations (U.N.) were made. The representatives wrote a constitution which was called the Charter of the United Nations. It was signed in June. The U.N. officially began on October 24, 1945. The headquarters was established in New York.

Goals of the U.N.

primary
(the most important)

maintain
(to keep)

The primary goal is to maintain international peace. The U.N. is also concerned with equal rights and self-government in countries. It also tries to solve economic and social problems in the world.

The Organization of the U.N.

The U.N. has six departments. The first department is the **Security Council.** It has five permanent members: China, France, Great Britain, Russia and the U.S. Ten other members are elected for two year terms. The Security Council tries to prevent wars. It has a military force to help keep peace.

The **General Assembly** has representatives from all U.N. members. It discusses world problems and makes recommendations.

The **Economic and Social Council** has fifty-four members who are elected for three years by the General Assembly. This council studies social, health, and cultural problems in the world.

133

The Security Council

The **Trusteeship Council** has members who are elected by the General Assembly. It helps colonies to become independent countries.

The **International Court of Justice** is also known as the World Court. It is located in the Netherlands. Fifteen judges are elected by the General Assembly and the Security Council. The judges solve legal problems between countries.

The **Secretariat** manages the U.N. The manager is called the **Secretary General.** The first Secretary-General was Trygve Lie of Norway. Other Secretary-Generals were Dag Hammarskjold of Sweden, U Thant of Burma, and Kurt Waldheim of Austria. Since 1982, Javier Perez de Cuellar of Peru has been the Secretary-General.

The U.N. and the Korean War
The U.N. tries to prevent war. In 1950, however, the U.N. became involved in a war. The war was in Korea which was a country in eastern Asia. After World War II, Korea became a divided country. In 1948, North and South Korea established two separate governments.

In June 1950, North Korea invaded South Korea. The U.N. sent an international army to stop the invader and to restore peace. Most of the soldiers in the U.N. army were from the U.S. The U.N. military was led by **General Douglas MacArthur** from the U.S. The Korean War lasted almost three years. Finally, in 1953, an agreement was reached. An armistice was signed. This agreement recognized the two countries of North Korea and South Korea.

Summary
After World War II, many countries were afraid of another world war. In order to prevent another world war, they formed the United Nations. The U.N. tries to maintain world peace, however, it sometimes becomes involved in wars.

VOCABULARY EXERCISE
Read these verbs. Use the endings "er" or "ative" to make nouns. These endings mean "a person".

1. lead _____ a person who leads

2. invade _____ a person who invades

3. represent _____ a person who represents

4. manage _____ a person who manages

Find the words in the reading passage. Circle them.

COMPREHENSION EXERCISE.
Answer the questions.

1. Which four countries met in 1944 to plan a peace organization?

_____

2. List three goals of the U.N.

_____

_____

_____

3. How many members does the Security Council have?

_____

4. What does the Security Council do?

_____

_____

5. Where is the U.N. located?

_____

6. Why did the U.N. enter the Korean War?

_____

_____

_____

_____

135

7. Do you think the U.N. and the Security Council help world peace? Why or why not?

_____

_____

_____

_____

GRAMMAR EXERCISE.

PASSIVE VOICE

Verbs can be in the **active voice** or in the **passive voice.** If the subject performs the action, the verb is in the active voice.
Example: The representatives planned the U.N.

If the subject is acted upon, the verb is in the passive voice.
Example: The U.N. was planned by the representatives.

The passive voice is formed with "be + the past participle".

Sometimes the subject is not written. It is understood.
Example: The U.N. was planned.

A. Read the passage. Find three sentences in the passive voice. Copy them below.

1. _____

_____

2. _____

_____

3. _____

_____

B. Rewrite the sentences in the passive voice.

1. The representatives held meetings.

   _____

2. The representatives made plans.

   _____

3. The countries called the organization the U.N.

   _____

4. North Korea invaded South Korea.

   _____

5. The U.N. sent an army.

   _____

6. MacArthur led the U.N. army.

   _____

7. The countries signed an agreement.

   _____

8. The agreement recognized two countries.

   _____

C. Write a sentence in the active voice. Rewrite it in the passive voice. Use the information in this lesson.

Active: _____

_____

_____

Passive: _____

_____

_____

GRAPHICAL LITERACY.
Look at the chart. Answer the questions.

UNITED NATIONS AGENCIES

UNITED NATIONS CAPITAL DEVELOPMENT FUND (UNCDF)
Loans money to developing countries for roads, schools, etc.

UNITED NATIONS INSTITUTE FOR TRAINING AND RESEARCH (UNITAR)
Provides training and research to help world peace

UNITED NATIONS CHILDREN'S FUND (UNICEF)
Has special programs which provide medical and educational services to children

UNITED NATIONS CONFERENCE ON TRADE AND DEVELOPMENT (UNCTAD)
Helps international trade.

UNITED NATIONS DISASTER RELIEF OFFICE (UNDRO)
Provides assistance to countries which have disasters, such as hurricanes, floods, and famine.

UNITED NATIONS HIGH COMMISSIONER FOR REFUGEES (UNHCR)
Provides legal and political protection for refugees. Assists in refugee resettlement.

UNITED NATIONS EDUCATIONAL, SCIENTIFIC, AND CULTURAL ORGANIZATION (UNESCO)
Helps to plan educational, scientific, and cultural programs among countries.

OTHER AGENCIES

1. How many agencies are listed in the diagram? _____

2. Are these the only U.N. agencies? _____

3. Which agency loans money to developing countries?

_____

4. Which agency helps refugees?

_____

5. Which agency provides medical and educational assistance to children?

_____

6. Which agency helps countries to plan educational systems?

_____

7. What does UNITAR mean?

_____

8. What does UNCTAD do?

_____

138

WRITING ACTIVITY.
Answer the questions with complete sentences.

1. The United Nations has many goals. Which one do you think is the most important?

_____

_____

2. Identify three reasons why this goal is important to you.

_____

_____

_____

Describe why the U.N. is important. Use your answers to the above questions to write a paragraph. The title should be: The Most Important U.N. Goal.

_____

_____

_____

_____

_____

_____

_____

_____

_____

_____

_____

_____

_____

REVIEW EXERCISE.
Do you remember the meaning of the following words?
United Nations, Security Council, General Assembly, Secretary General, Korean War

UNIT REVIEW
Describe the importance of each person, place, document, or event.

1. the New Deal

_____

_____

2. Franklin Delano Roosevelt

_____

_____

3. World War II

_____

_____

4. the Allies

_____

_____

5. Hiroshima and Nagasaki

_____

_____

6. United Nations

_____

_____

7. Korean War

_____

_____

IMPORTANT TIMES
Write the important event that happened in each of these years.

Dec. 7, 1941 _____

1941-1945 _____

May 7, 1945 _____

Aug. 6 and Aug. 9, 1945 _____

Sept. 2, 1945 _____

Oct. 24, 1945 _____

UNIT FIVE

THE COUNTRY PROSPERS

THE STRUGGLE FOR CIVIL RIGHTS

THE U.S. TODAY

THE COUNTRY PROSPERS

PERSONAL SURVEY
Discuss these questions with your teacher and class.

1. Do you live in a city, in a suburb, in a town, or in a rural area?
2. How old do you think your community is?
3. What do you do with your free time?
4. What do your parents do with their free time?

PRE-READING

During the 1950's, the U.S. had good times. Many people were doing very well. The country was growing rapidly. There were many new jobs and the U.S. was enjoying peace with other countries. You will read about the prosperous times in the 1950's in this lesson.

CONTENT VOCABULARY
These words are important in this lesson. What do you know about them?

Dwight D. Eisenhower
Dr. Jonas Salk
Explorer I

SURVEY
Read the first paragraph, the subtitles, the words in bold print, and the summary. Look at the pictures.

1. How did life change during the 1950's?

Look at the comprehension questions. Try to find the answers to these questions when you read the passage.

THE COUNTRY PROSPERS

prosper
(to have
better
conditions)

The U.S. was at peace during the 1950's. Life became better for many Americans.

The Baby Boom

During the 1950's, the population of the U.S. increased by more than twenty-eight million. There were two reasons for this rapid increase. First, immigration increased. Second, many soldiers who had returned from World War II and the Korean War got married and started families. This period was called **The Baby Boom** because many babies were born during this time.

During this time, many cities grew. Many unemployed came to the cities to find jobs. **Suburbs** also began to grow. Many people who worked in the large cities moved to the suburbs. These people wanted to buy their own houses. They wanted yards in which their children could play. By 1960, more than 85% of the total U.S. population growth was in the suburbs.

A family buys their first TV

Life Improves for Many Americans

In the early 1950's, Americans began to have more free time. The average work week decreased to forty hours per week. The average length of a paid vacation was two weeks. Many American families who had their own cars wanted to travel on their vacations. Many American families traveled to national parks. Many went camping and fishing. Motels, gas stations, large highways, and fast food restaurants appeared in all parts of the country.

convention
(a meeting)

Television became very popular. Many people bought black and white televisions. Color TV was invented during the 1950's, but most people did not buy color televisions until the 1960's. In 1952, the first political conventions were on TV. Many Americans saw a political convention for the first time. They watched the political parties choose their presidential candidates. People also watched the news. They began to see events happening in the country.

Progress in Science

Many new medicines were developed in the 1950's. These medicines cured and prevented some diseases which killed many people. **Penicillin** was one of the more important medicines which became widely used in the 1950's. It was used to treat many diseases. Polio was a terrible disease which crippled and killed many people, especially children. In fact, President Roosevelt was crippled by polio in the 1920's. In 1955, **Dr. Jonas Salk** produced a vaccine which prevented polio. During the same year, thousands of school children received the **polio vaccine.** Shortly thereafter, there were very few new cases of polio in the U.S.!

Dwight D. Eisenhower,
President of the United States,
1953-1961

Eisenhower Becomes President

In 1952, President Truman did not run for re-election. General Dwight D. Eisenhower ran for the Republican Party and Adlai E. Stevenson ran for the Democratic Party. General Eisenhower was a World War II military leader who had led the U.S. army in Europe. He was very popular. He won the election in 1952 and was re-elected in 1956.

Space Exploration Begins

On October 4, 1957, Russia sent the first satellite into space. The U.S. worked very hard to develop its own space program. On January 31, 1958, the U.S. launched its first satellite into orbit around the earth. This satellite was called the **Explorer I.** This was the beginning of the U.S. space program!

Summary

There were many changes in the U.S. after World War II. The population grew rapidly. People had more free time. Medicines were developed to treat many diseases. The 1950's was a good period for many people in the U.S.

VOCABULARY EXERCISE.

A. Read these verbs. Make nouns by adding "tion".

VERBS	NOUNS
1. elect	_____
2. explore	_____
3. convene	_____
4. re-elect	_____

B. Write the correct form of the nouns or verbs in these sentences.

1. Representatives from many states _____ every four years to choose a presidential candidate.

2. Americans _____ Eisenhower President in 1952.

3. Space _____ began in the 1950's.

4. Americans _____ Eisenhower in 1956.

COMPREHENSION EXERCISE.
Answer the questions.

1. Why were the early 1950's called "The Baby Boom"?

_____

_____

2. Why did people move from the cities to the suburbs?

_____

_____

3. Why did Americans have more free time?

_____

_____

4. What was one popular invention of the 1950's? Describe how it changed Americans' lives.

_____

_____

5. What new vaccine was produced? Why was it important?

_____

_____

6. What did Eisenhower do before he became President?

_____

_____

7. When was the beginning of the U.S. space program?

_____

_____

8. Do you think space exploration is important? Why or why not?

_____

_____

GRAMMAR EXERCISE

> **CONNECTORS**
>
> The connectors **who** and **which** can connect sentences.
> **Which** refers to things.
>
> **Who** refers to people.

A. Read the passage. Find a sentence with ''who'' and a sentence with ''which''. Copy them below.

1. who _____

_____

2. which _____

_____

B. Combine the sentences. Use ''who'' or ''which''.

1. Many people moved to the cities.

   The people were unemployed.

_____

_____

2. People moved from the cities to towns.

   The towns were called suburbs.

   _____

   _____

3. People took vacations.

   The vacations lasted two weeks.

   _____

   _____

4. Television was an important invention.

   Television changed American life.

   _____

   _____

5. Polio was a terrible disease.

   Many people died from polio.

   _____

   _____

6. Adlai Stevenson was a Democrat.

   Adlai Stevenson ran for President in 1952.

   _____

   _____

C. Write two sentences. Write one with ''which'' and another with ''who''. Use the information from this lesson.

1. who _____

   _____

   _____

2. which _____

   _____

   _____

GRAPHICAL LITERACY.
Look at the chart. Answer the questions.

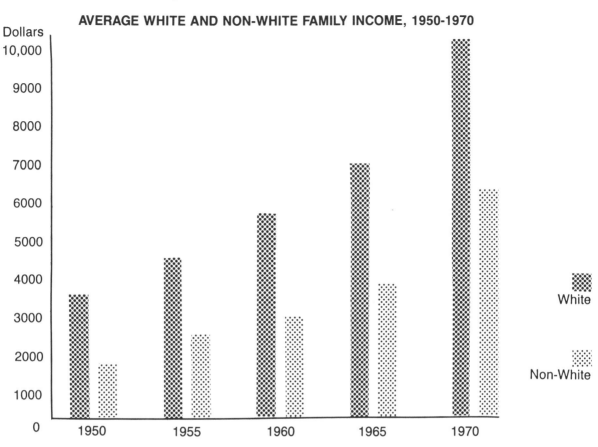

AVERAGE WHITE AND NON-WHITE FAMILY INCOME, 1950-1970

1. Which years does the chart cover? _____

2. What is shown on the side of the chart? _____

3. What does the black bar indicate? _____

4. What does the light bar indicate? _____

5. What was the average white family income in 1970? _____

6. What was the average non-white family income in 1970? _____

7. What was the average white family income in 1950? _____

8. What was the average non-white family income in 1950? _____

9. What was the average white family income in 1960? _____

10. What was the average non-white family income in 1960? _____

11. What was the approximate increase in white income between 1950 and 1960? _____

12. What was the approximate increase in non-white income between 1950 and 1960?

_____

WRITING ACTIVITY.
Answer the questions with complete answers.

1. Identify three reasons why living in a city is good.

_____

_____

_____

2. Identify three reasons why living in a suburb is good.

_____

_____

_____

Pretend that you have friends or family who are immigrating to the U.S. They do not know if they should move to a city or to the suburbs. Write them a letter. Make a suggestion about where they should live.

Dear _____,

_____

_____

_____

_____

_____

_____

_____

_____

_____

                                        Sincerely,

                                        _____

REVIEW EXERCISE.
Do you remember the meaning of the following words?
Baby Boom, suburbs, polio vaccine, Explorer I

THE STRUGGLE FOR CIVIL RIGHTS

PERSONAL SURVEY
Discuss these questions with your teacher and class.

1. What rights do you have?
2. Do all people have the same rights?
3. If some people do not have the same rights as others, what should they do?

PRE-READING

During the 1950's and 1960's, Black Americans and other minorities worked very hard to obtain the same rights that other Americans had. You will read about the struggle for equal rights in this lesson.

CONTENT VOCABULARY
These words are important in this lesson. What do you know about them?

Brown vs. The Board of Education
Martin Luther King, Jr.
Coretta Scott King
Civil Rights Acts
John F. Kennedy
Lyndon Johnson

SURVEY
Read the first paragraph, the subtitles, the words in bold print, and the summary. Look at the pictures.

1. Which laws were passed?
2. Who was the leader of the Civil Rights Movement?
3. Which Presidents worked for Civil Rights?

Look at the comprehension questions. Try to find the answers to these questions when you read the passage.

THE STRUGGLE FOR CIVIL RIGHTS

struggle (a strong effort) The 1950's were basically good years for many people in the U.S. However, Black Americans and other minorities were discriminated against. They struggled to obtain equal rights. The **Civil Rights Movement** was a very important part of modern U.S. history.

Segregation

discriminate (to deny equal rights) Black Americans were **discriminated** against in many parts of the U.S. Black children often had to go to separate schools. The back seats in buses were reserved for Blacks—they could not sit in the front. Public places had separate restrooms and drinking fountains for Blacks. In addition, Blacks often had to meet special requirements in order to vote. In fact, these requirements were designed to prevent Blacks from voting.

The Civil Rights Movement Begins

In 1954, the Supreme Court made an important decision. The Supreme Court case was called "**Brown versus the Board of Education of Topeka, Kansas**". In their ruling, the Supreme Court said "**separate but equal**" school facilities were unconstitutional. Now Black children could go to the same schools as other children.

segregate (to separate) A Black woman named Rosa Parks helped to end the segregation on buses. In December, 1955, Mrs. Parks sat down in a bus seat marked "for whites". The bus driver asked her to move to the back of the bus. She refused. She was arrested. The next day **Dr. Martin Luther King,** a young Black minister, led a protest. More than 50,000 people boycotted the bus system! Later, the Supreme Court ruled the Alabama segregation laws unconstitutional.

In the late 1950's and early 1960's, there were many demonstrations. Many people marched. They carried signs which showed they wanted equal rights. Sometimes thousands of people would march for equal rights. These marches were organized by Black leaders such as Dr. Martin Luther King.

Dr. Martin Luther King leads a demonstration

Presidents Kennedy and Johnson Work For Civil Rights

John Kennedy was elected President in 1960. He worked hard for civil rights. He helped to guarantee voting rights to all Americans. In some states, Blacks had to pay a special tax in order to vote. Kennedy helped to create the **Twenty-Fourth Amendment** which prohibited this tax.

Lyndon Johnson became President after Kennedy was assassinated in November, 1963. The **Civil Rights Act** was passed in 1964. It removed all special registration requirements for voting. It also prohibited segregation in employment and housing. A government agency, the Equal Employment Opportunity Commission, was established to enforce the Civil Rights Act.

Dr. Martin Luther King Is Assassinated

Dr. Martin Luther King was the leader of the Civil Rights Movement. He led many demonstrations and marches throughout the country. On April 4, 1968, he was assassinated in Memphis, Tennessee. Other people, such as his wife Coretta Scott King, continued his work.

Summary

The Civil Rights Movement was very important during the 1950's and 1960's. Dr. Martin Luther King helped to obtain equal rights for minorities in the U.S. Furthermore, the work for equal rights still continues today.

AN IMPORTANT PERSON IN U.S. HISTORY: Dr. Martin Luther King

Dr. Martin Luther King was born on January 15, 1929 in Georgia. Both his father and grandfather were ministers. He went to college and studied religion. He became a minister. He married Coretta Scott and they had four children.

In 1955, he led a boycott to end segregation on buses in Montgomery, Alabama. He worked very hard for civil rights. He traveled around the country and gave many speeches. He led many marches and demonstrations. He helped to organize a major march in Washington D.C. on August 28, 1963. More than 200,000 people demonstrated for equal rights. They heard Dr. King's famous speech in which he said that "I have a dream that someday all men would be brothers".

In 1964, Dr. King received the Nobel Peace Prize. This is an international prize which is given every year to the most important person. Dr. King received the award because he worked peacefully to obtain equal rights. Dr. King did not believe in violence.

VOCABULARY EXERCISE
Read these words. Write the words next to their definitions.

| modern | to segregate | to discriminate | equal |
| a ruling | to arrest | to assassinate | to struggle |

1. _____ To murder a leader.

2. _____ To accuse someone of a crime and to put the person in jail.

3. _____ A decision by the Supreme Court.

4. _____ Recent.

5. _____ To separate.

6. _____ To deny someone equal rights.

7. _____ To work very hard to obtain something.

8. _____ The same.

COMPRHENSION EXERCISE.
Answer the questions.

1. What is segregation?

_____

_____

_____

2. What does "separate but equal" mean?

_____

_____

_____

3. What did Rosa Parks do?

_____

_____

4. Who was a Black leader that led a march in Montgomery, Alabama?

_____

_____

5. How did people obtain civil rights for minorities?

_____

_____

6. Why was the Civil Rights Act important?

_____

_____

_____

7. Do you think everyone in the U.S. liked the Civil Rights movement? Why or why not?

_____

_____

_____

GRAMMAR EXERCISE.

CONNECTING WORDS join ideas.

They can introduce sentences.

A. Read the passage. Find sentences with "however", "in fact", "in addition", and "furthermore".

1. however _____

_____

2. in fact _____

_____

3. in addition _____

_____

4. furthermore _____

_____

B. Complete the sentences with the correct connector. Use "in addition", "however", "in fact", or "furthermore".

Dr. Martin Luther King led marches in the U.S. _____, he led boycotts which prevented people from using busses or shopping in stores. Dr. King led the movement for civil rights. _____, his demonstrations helped to get laws passed. Many rights for minorities were obtained during the 1950's. _____, the struggle for civil rights continues today.

C. Complete the sentences. Use the information from this lesson.

1. Dr. King led boycotts. In addition, _____

_____

_____

2. Dr. King worked hard for civil rights. In fact, _____

_____

_____

3. The Civil Rights Act prohibits segregation in housing. Furthermore, _____

_____

_____

4. Many laws were passed to guarantee equal rights. However, _____

_____

_____

D. Write two sentences with a connector. Use the information from this lesson.

1._____

_____

2._____

_____

GRAPHICAL LITERACY.
Look at the charts. Answer the questions.

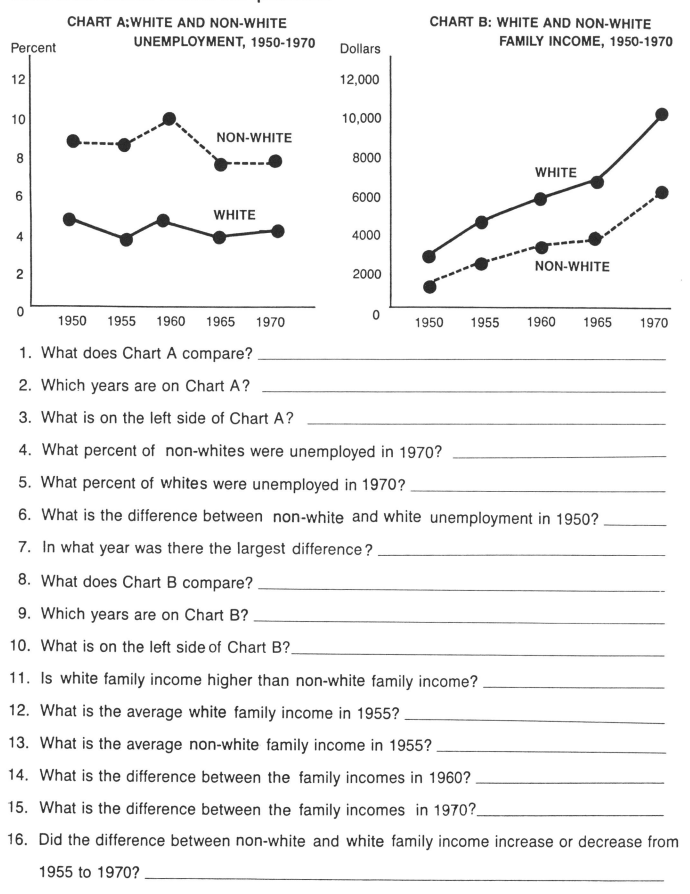

CHART A: WHITE AND NON-WHITE UNEMPLOYMENT, 1950-1970

Percent

CHART B: WHITE AND NON-WHITE FAMILY INCOME, 1950-1970

Dollars

1. What does Chart A compare? _____

2. Which years are on Chart A? _____

3. What is on the left side of Chart A? _____

4. What percent of non-whites were unemployed in 1970? _____

5. What percent of whites were unemployed in 1970? _____

6. What is the difference between non-white and white unemployment in 1950? _____

7. In what year was there the largest difference? _____

8. What does Chart B compare? _____

9. Which years are on Chart B? _____

10. What is on the left side of Chart B? _____

11. Is white family income higher than non-white family income? _____

12. What is the average white family income in 1955? _____

13. What is the average non-white family income in 1955? _____

14. What is the difference between the family incomes in 1960? _____

15. What is the difference between the family incomes in 1970? _____

16. Did the difference between non-white and white family income increase or decrease from

    1955 to 1970? _____

WRITING ACTIVITY.
Answer the questions with complete sentences.

1. List three laws which were made because of the Civil Rights Movement. How did each law change life in the U.S.?

_____

_____

_____

_____

Describe how the Civil Rights Movement changed your life. Use your answer to the above question to write a paragraph. The title should be: How the Civil Rights Movement Helped My Life.

_____

_____

_____

_____

_____

_____

_____

_____

_____

_____

_____

_____

_____

_____

_____

_____

REVIEW EXERCISE.
Do you remember the meaning of the following words?
Civil Rights Movement, Dr. Martin Luther King, Civil Rights Act, Twenty-Fourth Amendment, Brown versus the Board of Education of Topeka, Kansas

THE U.S. TODAY

PERSONAL SURVEY
Discuss these questions with your teacher and class.

1. What is a major problem in the U.S. today?
2. What is a major problem in the world?

PRE-READING

There are many problems which need to be solved. In this lesson you will read about some of the major problems and concerns in the U.S. today.

CONTENT VOCABULARY
These words are important in this lesson. What do you know about them?

drugs

AIDS

The Vietnam War

American Disabilities Act

Breakup of the U.S.S.R.

SURVEY
Read the first paragraph, the subtitles, the words in bold print, and the summary.

1. Which areas are discussed in the lesson?

Look at the comprehension questions. Try to find the answers to these questions when you read the passage.

THE UNITED STATES TODAY (1970 - 1993)

The United States continues to grow. There are many developments in health, science, education, and way of life. Although there has been a lot of progress, there continue to be many issues which Americans are concerned about.

Health

Americans have a longer life expectancy than before. The average man lives until the age of 71. The average woman lives until the age of 78. Heart disease and cancer are the two major causes of death. Smoking can cause both heart disease and lung cancer.

AIDS is a deadly disease. AIDS stands for "acquired immune deficiency syndrome". The disease is caused by a virus called HIV. The disease destroys the body's ability to protect itself from infection. The disease is spread primarily through sexual contact, use of infected hypodermic needles, or exchange of contaminated blood. There is no cure for this disease. A lot of research is needed to find a cure.

The use of drugs and alcohol is another problem. Drugs, such as crack, cocaine, and heroin, are very dangerous. People can become dependent on drugs. Sometimes they even die. Continual drinking of a lot of alcohol can lead to liver disease and other health problems. Many traffic accidents and deaths are caused by drivers who have been drinking.

Education

A primary and secondary education is free and available to everyone. There are many opportunities for persons to get an education. According to the 1990 census, over 78% of Americans had completed four years of high school.

Many people are concerned about the quality of education. Some students graduate high school without good reading, writing, or math skills. More than 15% of American adults are functionally illiterate. They do not have the basic skills needed for everyday living. Some cannot read their bills, write checks, or fill out job applications. Many special programs are available to help young adults and older adults to learn to read and write.

Equal Rights

Since the 1960's, many laws have been passed to guarantee equal rights to all U.S. citizens. Some of these laws prohibited discrimination in education and employment. These laws are trying to guarantee equal opportunity for all Americans.

In 1972, Congress passed the Equal Rights Amendment which guaranteed equal rights for women. However, it did not become an official amendment to the Constitution because it was not approved by the states. Because of the work for equal rights, more women entered business and government. In 1981, Sandra Day O'Connor was the first woman appointed to the U.S. Supreme Court. In 1984, Geraldine Ferraro, ran for vice-president of the U. S.

In 1990, the Americans with Disabilities Act (ADA) became a law. It prohibited discrimination against people with physical and mental disabilities. Equal rights are important for all Americans.

Energy

Much of the world's energy comes from oil. The U.S. buys much of its oil from other countries, especially those in the Middle East. People realize that oil will not always be available.

The U.S. is trying to find other sources of energy. One major source is nuclear power. Today many nuclear power plants are being built. Many people are concerned about the safety of these plants. People are afraid of the accidents and the problems that radioactivity can cause. In the 1980's, two major accidents happened. One accident happened at Three Mile Island in Pennsylvania. The other happened at Chernobyl, a nuclear power plant in Russia. Each accident demonstrated the power and seriousness of nuclear energy.

The Environment

People are polluting our **environment.** Smoke from chimneys and fumes from our cars pollute the air. Chemicals used to kill weeds pollute the soil. Sewage and waste water from factories pollute our rivers and oceans. This pollution is dangerous for plants, animals, and people.

People are trying to save the environment in many ways. One way is to **conserve** energy. You can save energy by using less electricity, oil, and gas. Another way to save the environment is to **recycle.** Instead of throwing away newspapers and magazines, you can recycle them. During recycling, the old paper is used to make new paper. An important way to save the environment is to pass laws which prohibit the destruction of our environment. One example is a law which prohibits companies or people from putting their sewage into the rivers.

Space

Since 1959, the U.S. has explored space. In 1969, two Americans landed on the moon. Since that time, the U.S. has placed into orbit many satellites for communication and television. Furthermore, space shuttle missions took place in the 1980's. Their goal was to start regular manned space flights. A terrible accident occurred in 1986. The space shuttle, Challenger, exploded and all the astronauts were killed.

Many new inventions have resulted from the space exploration program. The U.S. spends a lot of money for space exploration. Some people debate the value of exploring space when the money could be used to provide assistance to the poor, homeless, or sick.

Fall of Communism

In 1980, Ronald Reagan became President. President Reagan took a strong stand against Communism. After Ronald Reagan served two terms, his vice-president, George Bush, was elected President. During those twelve years, many countries turned from Communism to democracy and freed themselves from the Communist bloc. On Oct. 2, 1992, East Germany and West Germany united into one country. Even the U.S.S.R. (Union of Soviet Socialist Republics) disbanded on Dec. 25, 1991 to become many independent countries. Most countries set up democracies. Many of the new countries are having problems with this new form of government.

Major Wars in the World

The Vietnam War lasted a long time. In 1955, North and South Vietnam became separate countries. North Vietnam had a Communist government. South Vietnam was led by President Diem. North Vietnam trained soldiers to fight in South Vietnam. These soldiers were called the Viet Cong. The Diem government asked the U.S. for help. President Kennedy did not want Communism to spread to South Vietnam. So he sent weapons and military advisors to train the South Vietnamese.

The Vietnam War **escalated** in the mid 1960's. In 1965, North Vietnamese boats fired at an American Navy ship. President Johnson ordered U.S. planes to bomb North Vietnam. The Viet Cong attacked U.S. military bases in South Vietnam. The fighting grew worse. In 1970, the U.S. and South Vietnam attacked North Vietnamese forces in Cambodia and Laos.

Many Americans were against the war. There were many demonstrations in the U.S. against the war. Finally, peace talks began in 1973, although the fighting still continued. In 1975, the South Vietnamese government surrendered. On July 2, 1976, South and North Vietnam were officially reunited as the Socialist Republic of Vietnam.

The war was very bad. In Vietnam, cities and farmlands were destroyed. Hundreds of thousands of people had been killed or wounded. More than 57,000 Americans and 200,000 South Vietnamese died. Many refugees left Vietnam. There were also Laotian and Cambodian refugees. At one time, the U.S. government was spending about 45% of the national budget for the war. More than $200 billion was spent in fighting the war.

The **war with Iraq** occurred in 1990. In August, Iraq invaded Kuwait. For six months, diplomats from many countries tried to persuade Iraqi President Saddam Hussein to remove his army. In January 1991, the U.S. and its allies began an air and ground attack against Iraq. In February, the U.S. and its allies forced the Iraquis from Kuwait.

Today, there still is **conflict** in many parts of the world, such as the Middle East, the former Yugoslavia, the former Soviet Republics, and Africa. Peace is still an important issue.

The Threat of Nuclear War

After the U.S. used atomic bombs in World War II, Americans began to worry about the possibility of nuclear war. Such a war could lead to complete destruction of the entire world. In the early 1970's, the U.S. and the U.S.S.R. began to talk about limiting the number of nuclear weapons. In 1987, President Reagan and President Gorbachev of the U.S.S.R. signed an agreement to dismantle U.S. and Soviet missiles. Talks about reducing or eliminating nuclear weapons are taking place today because many countries still have large numbers of nuclear weapons. In addition, other countries, such as Iraq, which do not have nuclear weapons now are trying to build them. Many people in the U.S. and the entire world are very worried about a nuclear war or a nuclear accident.

The U.S. Today

The U.S. continues to grow and progress. However, there are many issues which Americans have to discuss and make decisions which will affect the future of the U.S. and the world. In 1993, Bill Clinton became the 42nd President of the U.S. He has a very difficult job. The U.S. is facing many problems both in the U.S. and in the world. In the past and in the present, the U.S. continues to be a nation of freedom, opportunity, and hope for many.

VOCABULARY EXERCISE.
Read these words. Write the words next to their definitions.

to conserve   to recycle   a conflict   the environment   to escalate

1. _____ the air, water, and land around us

2. _____ an argument or fight

3. _____ to grow

4. _____ to save

5. _____ to use again

COMPREHENSION EXERCISE.
Answer the questions.

1. How long does the average American man live? _____

2. How long does the average American woman live? _____

3. Why do you think the life expectancy is longer for a woman than for a man? _____

_____

4. What are the two major causes of death? _____

5. Why is AIDS a deadly disease? _____

_____

6. Why do you think education is important to the future of the U.S.? _____

_____

7. What are some sources of energy? _____

8. What can you do to save the environment? _____

_____

_____

9. How many years has the U.S. been involved in space exploration? _____

10. What happened to the U.S.S.R. in 1991? _____

_____

_____

11. Is there peace in the world today? _____

GRAPHICAL LITERACY.
Read the charts and the table. Answer the questions.

NUMBERS OF IMMIGRANTS TO THE U.S.: 1961 - 1990

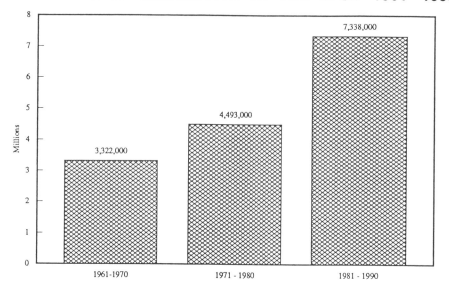

1. How many immigrants came between 1981 and 1990? _____

2. How many more immigrants came during 1981 - 1990 than during 1961 - 1970? _____

3. Do you think more or fewer immigrants will come to the U.S. between 1991 and 2000? _____

SOURCES OF IMMIGRANTS: 1981 - 1990

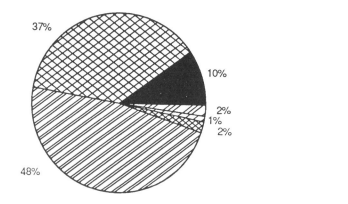

1. What percent of the immigrants came from Asia? _____

2. Where did most of the immigrants come from? _____

3. What percent of the immigrants came from North America, Central America, and South America? _____

LANGUAGES SPOKEN AT HOME

The 1990 Census asked Americans what languages they spoke at home. Most Americans speak English at home, but many Americans speak another language. The chart below shows the 12 states with the highest percentage of people who speak another language at home.

State	Percentage speaking another language at home	Four most popular languages
New Mexico	55%	Spanish, Navajo, Keres, Zuni
California	46%	Spanish, Chinese, Tagalog, Vietnamese
Texas	34%	Spanish, French, German, Vietnamese
Hawaii	33%	Japanese, Tagalog, Ilocano, Chinese
New York	31%	Spanish, Italian, Chinese, French
Arizona	26%	Spanish, Navajo, German, French
New Jersey	24%	Spanish, Italian, Polish, German
Rhode Island	21%	Portuguese, Spanish, French, Italian
Florida	21%	Spanish, French, Creole, German
Connecticut	18%	Spanish, Italian, French, Polish
Massachusetts	18%	Spanish, Portuguese, French, Italian
Illinois	17%	Spanish, Polish, German, Italian

1. Which state has the highest percentage of people who speak another language at home?

_____

2. Which language is popular in 11 of the 12 states? _____

3. Where is Vietnamese a popular language? _____

4. Where is Chinese a popular language? _____

5. In how many states is Polish a popular language? _____

6. In how many states is Navajo a popular language? _____

7. Look at the languages spoken in New Mexico. Who do you think speaks Navajo, Keres, and Zuni? _____

8. Is your state on the chart? _____   Is your native language on the chart? _____

WRITING EXERCISE.
Answer the questions with complete answers.

1. What do you think is the most important problem in the U.S. today?

_____

_____

2. Why is this problem important? Write at least three reasons.

_____

_____

_____

Use your answers to write a composition. The title should be: The Most Important Problem in the U.S. Today.

_____

_____

_____

_____

_____

_____

_____

_____

_____

_____

_____

_____

_____

_____

_____

_____

_____

UNIT REVIEW
Describe the importance of each person, document, or event.

1. Explorer I

_____

_____

2. Civil Rights Movement

_____

_____

3. Brown versus the Board of Education of Topeka, Kansas

_____

_____

4. Dr. Martin Luther King

_____

_____

5. Civil Rights Act of 1964

_____

_____

6. Vietnam War

_____

_____

7. American Disabilities Act

_____

_____

IMPORTANT TIMES
Write the important event that happened.

Jan. 31, 1958 _____

1960 _____

Nov. 22, 1963 _____

1964 _____

Apr. 4, 1968 _____

Dec. 25, 1991 _____